What a beautiful and honest story of faith, friendship, and transformation, all thanks to a chance encounter. We can all learn something from both the 104-year-old war hero and the forty-something journalist, both on a quest to leave the world better than they found it. There is something—a lesson, a truth, a question—for all of us in *Two Hundred Tuesdays*.

LAUREN FERRARA, journalist and founder of Why Wait Stories

The World War II generation left us a blueprint for how to be better people and how to coexist in a better world. Jim Downing is one of the many architects of that blueprint. Dianne Derby captures the true essence of this incredible man, who was there in the crucible of Pearl Harbor and went on to make sure we never forget December 7, 1941, and the lessons of that day, which still resonate in all our lives.

TIM GRAY, filmmaker and founder and president of the World War II Foundation

Dianne Derby once confidently faced her future with a headstrong tenacity. Then she met "Grandpa Jim," her life mentor. Raised in the Christian faith, Derby met Jesus in a fresh way thanks to this unlikely friendship. In *Two Hundred Tuesdays*, she reveals how Jim Downing's impact gave her the resources not simply to navigate life but also to enjoy life fully.

MARK CONFORTI, DMin, United Methodist pastor and author of *Clergy Mentoring*

Honest, vulnerable, and engaging. A beautiful picture of friendship and discipleship. A must-read!

DR. MARK MAYFIELD, counselor, speaker, coach, and author of *The Path out of Loneliness*

Dianne Derby's *Two Hundred Tuesdays* is a delightful, emotional guide of resiliency and perseverance filled with inspiring anecdotes of positivity and her perilous journey of self-discovery with an American hero as her mentor. I LOVED this book, a must-read for all empaths and anyone who's faced adversity, and also a gift to the world, filled with positive core values, self-love, and paying it forward. I can't wait to share this incredibly thoughtful book with my friends and family.

PHIL MARTINEZ, president and CEO of PM Productions

This is a book that captures a friendship across generations, across gender, and even across faith traditions. It is a gem of a book that reminds readers that sometimes Truth transcends. Dianne is a newscaster bent on finding and breaking the next big story. (She is very good at that, by the way.) Jim was an aging war hero who had The Story that just had to be shared. Put on the spot, Dianne unflinchingly took on the challenge, and the result is this charming book. Read it and be blessed.

DON PAPE, curator of Pape Commons

Dianne's faith journey is brutally honest, touching, and inspiring. Anyone who wants to know what it is like to walk humbly with God must read it!

VINH CHUNG, MD, author of *Where the Wind Leads*

Two Hundred Tuesdays: What a Pearl Harbor Survivor Taught Me about Life, Love, and Faith is much more than the story of a Pearl Harbor survivor; it's also a book about relationships, marriage, and lessons learned from Jim. Dianne's boldness to be authentic is captured immediately. This book will inspire kindness toward one another; I confidently recommend it for those wanting more out of life, love, and faith.

LARRY DOZIER, MBA, veteran and chairman of the board at Mt. Carmel Veterans Service Center

Accomplished people in their last stage of life are in a unique position to impart wisdom and understanding to those immersed in the day-to-day struggles of work, marriage, and child-rearing. *Two Hundred Tuesdays* is a great example of the healing power of such meaningful relationships between young and old.

JOHN SUTHERS, mayor of Colorado Springs

Two Hundred Tuesdays

Two

WHAT A PEARL HARBOR SURVIVOR TAUGHT ME

Hundred

ABOUT LIFE, LOVE, AND FAITH

Tuesdays

DIANNE DERBY

with T. L. Heyer

A NavPress resource published in alliance
with Tyndale House Publishers

NavPress is the publishing ministry of The Navigators, an international Christian organization and leader in personal spiritual development. NavPress is committed to helping people grow spiritually and enjoy lives of meaning and hope through personal and group resources that are biblically rooted, culturally relevant, and highly practical.

For more information, visit NavPress.com.

Two Hundred Tuesdays: What a Pearl Harbor Survivor Taught Me about Life, Love, and Faith

Copyright © 2022 by Dianne Derby. All rights reserved.

A NavPress resource published in alliance with Tyndale House Publishers

NavPress and the NavPress logo are registered trademarks of NavPress, The Navigators, Colorado Springs, CO. *Tyndale* is a registered trademark of Tyndale House Ministries. Absence of ® in connection with marks of NavPress or other parties does not indicate an absence of registration of those marks.

The Team:
David Zimmerman, Publisher; Caitlyn Carlson, Acquisitions Editor; Elizabeth Schroll, Copy Editor; Olivia Eldredge, Operations Manager; Ron C. Kaufmann, Designer

Unless otherwise indicated, cover images are the property of their respective copyright holders from Depositphotos, and all rights are reserved. Paper texture copyright © PicsFive; napkin copyright © koosen; stains copyright © bogalo; scratches copyright © Mioki; newspaper from Harvard library/Wikimedia; Jim Downing copyright © Brett B. Clark/The Navigators.org and used with permission.

Author photo by Don Jones, copyright © 2021. All rights reserved.

The author is represented by the literary agency of Word Serve Literary, www.wordserveliterary.com.

Some of the anecdotal illustrations in this book are true to life and are included with the permission of the persons involved. All other illustrations are composites of real situations, and any resemblance to people living or dead is purely coincidental.

For information about special discounts for bulk purchases, please contact Tyndale House Publishers at csresponse@tyndale.com, or call 1-855-277-9400.

ISBN 978-1-64158-373-2

Printed in the United States of America

28	27	26	25	24	23	22
7	6	5	4	3	2	1

To Claire and Chip:

May you know the peace

that surpasses all understanding.

—

CONTENTS

INTRODUCTION

WHAT DO YOU REMEMBER about the last newscast you watched? Since I work in a business that is driven by ratings, I sincerely hope you remember the news anchor at the desk—but the truth is, you probably don't.

You probably remember only one story. We are wired to crave stories, to value authenticity, to long for the truth. We want to know about tomorrow's forecast, crime in our community, and what's happening with the latest recall. We want to leave the newscast feeling okay enough about the world that we will come back and watch more tomorrow. That's why the final story in a newscast is usually a positive one.

Now you know the secret to broadcasting the news.

Like you, I usually only remember one story from each newscast. You know the kind—the story that tugs at your heartstrings. I never forget the sobs of the mother whose young daughter is missing, the sound of her voice as she begs her daughter to come home; the family huddled in a corner of a shelter after they evacuated their home when high winds whipped a fire into an inferno; or the widow who won't see her husband again.

Let's face it—I don't bring the good news; I tell you the bad. In newsrooms, we search for the sound bite that cuts straight to the heart of the matter, to the truth of someone's soul. That's what makes television news compelling. Until you hear the story firsthand from the person most impacted, you can't really get it. Journalists are trained to find those ten-second, meaningful sound bites, because those ten seconds are the reason you watch.

Because I am a journalist, I tell stories for a living. I don't make things up, and nothing I report is fiction. I'm a truth-teller, and I present each story as it happened—even if it's hard to say, hard to hear. I chase after authenticity. When I interview someone, I expect them to tell the truth. Without truth and authenticity, what can we really hold on to?

There's a dichotomy in journalism, though. Because I am a journalist, I have been taught not to share my own emotions, and I'll be honest with you about that too: This part of the work is hard for me. Growing up, my nickname was "Teary" because I cried all the time. I cried over the things that made me sad, and I cried over the things that made other people sad.

I finally found a word for all of this in my forties: *empath*. My dear friend Alyssa sent me an article about people with this trait and said, "Derbs, I think this is you."

I read the article over and over, feeling so understood for the first time. An empath feels everything, including others' emotions *as if they were their own*. Sometimes the stories I report are enough to tear me in half. Sometimes I want to cry on the air, and it feels inauthentic to hold back. How can I not show what I'm feeling?

For seventeen years, I have been trained to show just enough emotion, but not too much. To share my thoughts, but not too much. To react to the interview sound bite, but not too much. The feedback I have heard time and time again? "Dianne, stop being so much."

But that's the problem: I simply *am* too much. How can one who is TOO MUCH not react too much? This is the balancing act of my life.

Everyone longs to be known, to be seen, to be heard. This basic need is right up there with oxygen, food, and shelter. When someone listens to you—truly wants to see who you are—well, that kind of knowing can change you.

That's what happened to me when Jim Downing came into my life: He saw me. He wanted to know me. He taught me a path to a life where my TOO MUCH found its home.

So in the pages of this book, I am coming as myself. My whole self. I want to show you who I am, and I want to show you who Jim was.

This is my story—and the story of the man who changed my life.

CHAPTER 1

A MILLION CHANCES TO SAY YES

A New Job, a New Haircut, and a Whole New Image

WE AREN'T YET out of the South Carolina city when my eyelids start to feel heavy. I tend to get immediate symptoms of narcolepsy as soon as I start any road trip longer than twenty minutes. This cross-country drive to Colorado is going to be a drowsy one.

"Mom, I have to pull over. I can't drive."

"Seriously? Already?" she says.

"Sorry. You know how I am. I can't help it."

"Well, pull over then. I guess I'll be driving this whole trip."

We pull into the nearest gas station and switch seats,

with my husband, Pete, trailing in the car behind us. I know Pete isn't even remotely surprised.

The cars are packed to the ceiling with clothing, makeup, and jewelry. That's all I've brought with me. The rest will stay in storage until move-in day at our townhome under construction in Colorado Springs. Something tells me Pete is happy to be all alone, blasting his music in his Volkswagen Jetta. Nobody back there is telling him what to do. He has nothing to worry about but his obstructed rear view.

Mom takes the wheel, and I take our Chihuahuas, Lily and Rosebud, putting the girls in my lap as we hit the road again. A long drive for a fresh start.

I snap a picture of the sunset and post the obligatory Facebook status update that accompanies a major life change. I decide to include lyrics by singer Jason Aldean: "With a windshield sunset in your eyes, like a watercolored painted sky, you think heaven's doors have opened."[1]

Yes, heaven's doors are opening for me. I just don't see how wide yet.

Excitement and nervousness are similar emotions, and they have spun together as butterflies in my stomach. I'm not sure which one I feel more at any given moment.

My departure from my job was unpleasant and

unexpected. I'd been put in a situation where I felt like I had to choose my job or my integrity, and so I left with about fifteen minutes' notice. Call it a black-and-white decision, call it all or nothing—call it whatever you'd like. But in a moment of perfect clarity, I realized I hadn't been heard, I wasn't valued, and my voice had been silenced. I wasn't going to compromise my integrity for any position or amount of money.

Now I'm driving away, with the city I love and a hard piece of my story in the rearview mirror.

My fresh start is a full-time job as an evening anchor at a news station in Colorado Springs. I'll finally get to tell the stories that matter most to me. I won't have to go out on the crime beat or the consumer beat. Now I get to tell stories about people who have faced the hardest things, walked the darkest paths, and found life on the other side—"the overcoming beat," if you will. I love these stories best, and I sense that viewers are hungry for them too. If you are like me, you stare at the screen in awe, and you listen to these people who have overcome, and you want to ask them, "How did you do it? How can life ever be happy again after the tragedy you have experienced? How, how, how are you okay?" I am hungry for stories of victory, of people who know that life must go on.

After three days on the road, Mom, Pete, and I pull

our two-car caravan into the parking lot of the extended-stay hotel that Pete and I will call home for the next several months. The hotel is lovely, located where the mountains meet the interstate, a quick ten-minute drive to the KKTV 11 News studios.

Pete and I fill our room in record time as we unload all my clothing. Let's just say . . . the closet fills quickly. When the hotel staff see just how many clothes I've brought, they let me borrow one of those rolling carts to keep in the room. I have so much stuff—jewel tone dresses to wear on the air (no pastels, no prints, of course), evening gowns to wear to emcee events, and accessories to accent my outfits but not distract from the stories. (I do confess I love giant chandelier earrings, and I sneak those in sometimes.) I even purchase renter's insurance, just in case my wardrobe gets destroyed. It sounds silly, I know, but these details matter in the news industry. If a news anchor is poorly dressed, the trolls of the internet will gladly let everyone know.

Pete and I quickly learn to enjoy vacation amenities in our everyday lives. The staff offer us breakfast every morning, Pete enjoys happy hour at night, and our Chihuahuas learn to ride the elevator like city girls, their toenails clicking like high heels on the polished floor. Our new "home" is just what we need.

We explore our new city with wide eyes and wonder.

New restaurants, new people, new stories—and all in front of a Rocky Mountains backdrop. I start each day with a long look at the majesty of Pikes Peak. "Yep," I say, "this will work just fine."

—

In my first minutes on the job, I meet Barb, a boisterous lady with a roaring laugh you can hear throughout the building. Barb is very clearly in charge of who and what gets into the building, and she greets me quickly before she rushes to get my boss, Liz Haltiwanger.

Alone for a moment in the studio, I take a deep breath and look around at the lights, cameras, screens, and giant glass anchor desk, polished to shine. How strange for everything to be so quiet, even for a moment.

So this is where I'll be for the next five years, I think. *Or at least that's what my contract says.*

I hear Liz's ballet flats glide across the floor as she bustles toward me with a brisk walk and a welcoming smile. "Hello, Dianne. Hurry. You have a phone call with our image consultant in two minutes."

And that's how I learn—quickly and immediately!— that Liz doesn't waste time, and she speaks and listens at double time speed. Liz does everything fast, and I swear her thoughts roll in ten-second-interview sound bites. She runs the newsroom, and she has too much to do to even think about slowing down. I match her stride, and we hit the ground running. She whisks me into the newsroom, ushers me into an editing booth, and launches me into a phone call with the image guru.

Now, let me say this: I usually like working with consultants. Newsroom staff typically complain about them, their big ideas, and their bossy tone when they arrive to tell you everything you're doing wrong. But I've learned to smile, listen, take the advice I want to use, smile again, and thank them. They're not always kind, but I've held on to some golden nuggets from them over the years.

Something is different about this consultant, though: She feels like a friend to me—which is good because she's about to redo my image with a sparkly coat of fresh paint. She quickly becomes the honest sister who will tell me if my makeup foundation is too light or too dark, if I have lipstick on my teeth, or if my smile looks fake. She studies my taped on-air test with my coanchor, and she says I look washed-out on TV. She tells me I need brighter lipstick and more eyeliner. She sends me to get a few inches cut off my hair, and she forwards me a picture of NBC anchor Amy Robach. "See those voluminous layers, Dianne? We need those on you."

I can do all of that. I even have Velcro rollers that

will do the trick. I go to the hair salon the next day, and I stop by Sephora and buy the brightest red lipstick I can find.

Lipstick. Eyeliner. Haircut. Layers. Check, check, check, check.

I spend most of my first days watching the newscast, improving my "look," and learning how things work at this station. The producers help create a Facebook fan page for me, and they start posting updates announcing that I'll be on-air soon. The local print reporter for the *Gazette* comes by to interview me for a quick article about my pending debut on KKTV, and the studio records promotional commercials. The consultant evaluates my new image and gives me a thumbs-up. New and improved, rebranded and remarketed, Dianne Derby is ready to go on the air.

My coanchor, Don Ward, is a seasoned journalist with multiple Emmys, and he can write stories faster than anyone I've ever known. He is quick-witted and brutally honest, and I immediately trust his wealth of experience by my side. We hit it off as coanchors, and he claims he told my managers to hire me. He says he's the reason I got the job.

Our consultants plan an anchor retreat that Don teasingly calls "Trust-Fall Camp," complete with ice-breaker activities meant to bond Don and me. We need to fast-forward our chemistry on set, to appear as if we have known each other for years.

I become his best audience in the newsroom; Don can poke fun at anything, and I laugh at everything. He is sarcastic, intelligent, and a wizard with words, and he absolutely goes bonkers in the newsroom over a grammar mistake on the air. The man knows his work well. Our bosses say I'm his equal, but I feel like I'll never catch up.

My first on-air moment is with a soldier surprising his daughters on our news set. He had been deployed and now wants to share his return with the world. That means as the viewers and I finally meet each other, I get to greet them with a happy story: a hero reunited with his family. Mine is now a voice they'll hear in their living rooms at night, and I pray they keep coming back to me for more. We're off and running this new leg of the race.

Only two months into my new job, the Waldo Canyon Fire ignites just west of Colorado Springs. I have never even heard of Waldo Canyon, the Flying W Ranch, Glen Eyrie, or Mountain Shadows, a neighborhood that lies in the path of the flames. The city is at risk of being consumed by fire.

I have never covered wildfires before, and everything feels scary, new, and profound. Don is out of town, so I am alone on the set when our general manager directs me to get on the air. General managers usually do not show up for breaking news—that's how big of a disaster Colorado Springs is facing. It's time to sink or swim. I hope I look presentable, but sweat covers me from the chest down. My dress is soaking wet by the end of the day.

I tread water for the next five days, covering stories on the air for sixty hours in a week, five twelve-hour shifts. I report evacuations of thirty-two thousand residents and the destruction of more than three hundred homes as the station stays on-air for a total of one hundred twenty hours. It's absolutely nuts. The breaking news comes in faster than anyone can update with a teleprompter. I ad-lib for five days. I have never done anything like this in my career. I feel as though I were flying blindly through the air, not knowing what's coming next but knowing I have to stay calm. This is my moment to lead the community as a trusted voice, someone they can rely on.

The fire continues to burn for a few weeks, but it does most of its destruction in just one day. I interview people who lost their homes, standing in the rubble of their properties. I try to offer any bit of comfort to these families whose possessions have been reduced to ash. Charred chimneys and only occasional houses that survived the flames are scattered about the neighborhoods. There are so many questions and so few answers, and so much heartache. People scour the depths of their exposed basements, looking for anything that survived, like a coffee mug that could withstand the temperatures. Our chief photojournalist, Mike, invites us to join him for both sides of his story—as police officers shout for him to evacuate with his family, and then when he returns to the skeleton of his home. Every story wrenches my heart.

Once the baptism of the Waldo Canyon Fire is over, nothing seems stressful on-air anymore. Lots of community requests start rolling in for the new journalist in town. I get invitations to events and parades, am asked to make appearances at every fundraising event in town, and am offered opportunities to emcee galas and balls. It is nonstop. Emails, letters, and phone calls come every day, and Liz coaches me in the fast pace of my new role.

She says, "Dianne, let's get your name out there. I want you to do as many events as you can so you can get a lot of visibility, but don't get burned out. You still have several obligatory events we'll expect you to do, too, like anchoring nearly every weekend of the Broncos season. That nonprofit who asked you to emcee their gala . . . Yep, that's a good one. Just know they'll expect you every year after. Say yes to everything you want to say yes to."

Ask and you shall receive, Liz. I'm a people pleaser, I'm married with no children, and I have time.

Before I know it, the open hours before my workday—from 7:00 a.m. until 2:00 p.m.—are filled with emcee events. I'm busy at luncheons and functions as many as four days a week. My coworkers keep warning me, "Don't let it consume your life," but I don't care what they say. Ultimately, each event brings someone special into my life, gives me an invaluable contact, and offers me a chance to become more closely connected with the community. So I say yes.

Dinner request? Yep.

Go to the top of Pikes Peak for a story? Yep.

Emcee this fund-raiser? Host that celebration? Attend this luncheon? Yep, yep, and yep.

I say yes to everything, and my boss approves it all. I'm always packed, ready, and mic'd up for the next thing. I burn every wick I have, run as fast as I can, and still I am starving for more. I have very little margin and even less rest, but I know this is my chance. I'll sleep later, in another life stage. For now, the answer will always be yes.

I have no way of knowing it yet, but the very best yes is just up ahead.

CHAPTER 2

TAKE ME TO CHURCH

What Have I Gotten Myself Into?

"Dianne, we have another invite for you. A bunch of World War II vets will be at a local diner, and the organizer informs us that one of oldest living survivors of Pearl Harbor will be there."

"I'm in," I say. A chance for a meet-and-greet with a hero—that's all I need to know. I decide to take our chief photojournalist, Mike, with me, just in case I can get a few minutes with this man who has seen so much.

The cozy little strip mall diner is crowded with silver-haired seniors wearing veterans hats, medals, and ribbons. I wait inside the door for a glimpse of

Jim Downing, knowing I stand out with my big hair and bright-pink lipstick. The white-haired, ninety-nine-year-old man walks into the restaurant wearing a dapper wool coat and steady dignity, even as he leans on his walker.

My first thought is, *Wait, did he drive here alone?* My first impression, I'll later realize, is the right one: Jim Downing is tender and fierce, a spry old man filled with a million surprises.

I introduce myself, extending my hand to shake his. "Jim Downing, what a joy to meet you. My name is Dianne Derby, and I'm here with KKTV 11 News. I wonder if I could do a quick interview with you, sir?"

His hands are big but gentle. He's not trying to one-up me with a firm handshake, like so many do, dwarfing my hand to make me feel intimidated in the presence of his power and strength. His blue eyes sparkle behind his glasses when he smiles. "Why, yes. Yes, of course."

We step into a corner of the diner's foyer, not even sitting down at a table, a fact that embarrasses me in hindsight. But the man is so intentional and present, it doesn't occur to me that he may want to sit down. He's just ready to go, right here, right now.

Plus I am a deliberate journalist, and I know how to get the sound bite we need for the evening news.

I'm not insincere, just pressed for time. I fit many interviews into one day, and Jim Downing is just one of many that will be featured on our newscast in just a few hours.

I squeeze in as many questions as I can, with Mike's camera rolling over my shoulder, nearly next to my face. We always want the person interviewed to look almost directly at the camera, but not quite.

"Jim, Pearl Harbor survivors are some of America's greatest heroes. I wonder, what is your reaction to that word?"

He immediately deflects the spotlight, shifting the conversation away from himself. He says, "Today's troops are the true heroes. I only dealt with a battle for a little while. The men and women today are under constant attack overseas."

Veterans are heroes to their core, and they have seen horrors we cannot imagine. It is not uncommon for a war veteran to deflect the conversation away from his experience—but this is different. Jim is not only turning the attention away from himself but also shining the spotlight on those he believes are more deserving. What a humble answer from this man who survived one of the worst attacks in American history. He won't take the moment for himself.

It is so quick and so fast, but Jim gives me the sound

bite I need. That's what I am after, so Mike turns off the camera. Task complete.

The interview is over, but I want more. One sentence? How could that be enough? The newscast may only allow for ten seconds of conversation, but I want to know more of his story.

"Thank you, Jim," I say, shaking his hand again. "This interview could never do your story justice, but you'll see it tonight on the news. I hope you'll watch." I feel so rushed, so insincere, knowing this man's war story deserves an hour-long newscast, not the ten-second sound bite he will receive. But this is the nature of TV news. On to the next story.

But if there were a soundtrack for my first conversation with Jim, this is where you would hear the record scratch. Everything stops for a moment, and I can't explain why. The air feels different around me. There is a magnetic quality to this man, and I know, somehow, that this won't be a one-time meeting.

He says, "Dianne, it's been a pleasure. Please email me. I'd like to stay in contact with you."

And then Jim reaches into his coat pocket and pulls out a business card, of all things. He's ninety-nine years old, retired for more than three decades—and yet he has a business card with an email address on it. (I suppose it's technically a calling card, since he is thirty years retired from business. But that is my first indication that Jim Downing will never truly be finished working until his life is over.)

His card is still in my wallet today, more than a decade later.

I email Jim later that day, expecting that my message will go straight to a folder that nobody ever reads. To my surprise, he replies immediately, inviting me to continue the conversation over lunch. So he's tech-savvy, too, this business-card-carrying, promptly emailing new friend of mine who can drive himself all over town, even as he approaches his hundredth birthday. I'm fascinated all the more.

I read his email and smile at my screen. *Lunch with Jim Downing . . . why not? I mean, it's not a news story, but it's a story I want to know.* I type my reply: "I'd love to join you."

Just after the email leaves my in-box with a digital whoosh, I hear the ping of an immediate reply.

"Bring your husband," he had written.

And with that, we have a date.

———

The Garden of the Gods Club is a high-end, elegant restaurant with sweeping views of the gorgeous Garden of the Gods, a magnificent red-rock landscape that has captivated me from the moment I moved to Colorado Springs. When Pete and I arrive, I spot Jim sitting with his son at a table for four, and I suddenly feel a twisting anxiety. Pete is gracious to join me for occasional business lunches like this one, but I know intuitively that this won't be a quick bite to eat.

Also, and more honestly, Pete and I both know that this guy is one of the founding members of The Navigators, a worldwide Christian ministry.[1] (I had done some research for this second conversation.) It suddenly occurs to me: *Jim is probably going to talk a lot about God, a topic Pete and I rarely discuss. This could get awkward.*

Sure enough, even before the server brings our salads, his son skips past the pleasantries and goes straight for the jugular. "Pete, Dianne, tell me about your relationship with Christ."

I reach for my glass of water and take a long swallow. My mind races.

Excuse me? What in the world? Are you kidding me? So THIS is how this meal is going to go. How could he lead with such a personal question? Unbelievable.

I feel exposed, horrified, and—quite frankly—annoyed. I look at Jim, thinking he, too, will be embarrassed at such a forward question, but he's waiting, smiling warmly, his eyes twinkling. He's curious to hear my response. I look at Pete, but he's looking right back at me, his unblinking eyes reminding me that he did not sign up for this.

So I take another small sip of my water, buying as much time as I can.

"Well," I say, slowly setting down my water glass. "I'm not sure how to answer that. I am Catholic."

I lay it there, as if it answers everything his son has asked. But Jim smiles and waits for me to say more, so I take another step down this unknown path.

I say, "I mean, I know God exists, and I believe he is part of my heart, but I can't say I have 'a relationship' with him." I can hear the air quotes in my own sentence.

The silence is thick as we wait through a long pause from these men. I can feel Pete shutting his mouth even tighter, watching the exchange like a game of ping-pong. *This is going to be a long lunch*, I think.

I want so badly to scramble with an excuse to leave, to get up from the pretty table and slip into the bathroom and right out the door. I could shoot off a quick email later to say a giant No Thank You to this bait-and-switch evangelism lunch. I absolutely cannot deal with evangelists and their pushy agenda. How can I make a smooth exit?

I want to say, "The God I know doesn't force feelings

down my throat." But instead, I take another sip of my water and decide I'll just eat as fast as I can and get on with the day.

Jim's smile is my only saving grace. Somehow I don't get up, and I don't storm out. I power through because I really want to get to know Jim. There is wisdom in this man that I want to know.

But I can tell you right now, I would have bolted away from anyone else who'd pressed with these questions. It was feeling too similar to a pushy consultant—the kind I don't entirely enjoy—swooping in with their advice to make me sparkle and shine.

But something about Jim's kind presence keeps drawing me in. From Jim, I feel only love.

Jim breaks the silence and looks at both Pete and me. He asks a much gentler question: "Do you want to see someone totally fulfilled?"

I nearly exhale aloud in relief. *Finally*, I think. *Jim, thank you for changing the subject!* This, I can handle. If Jim has a lead for another story for me, then we can leave all this God business behind on the cutting room floor.

"Sure!" I say with audible enthusiasm, directing all my attention to Jim.

"You're looking at him," he says.

I gasp internally. *What does that even mean?*

I stare at this man I've known for a total of maybe one hour. I wonder how that's even possible—for anyone to claim to be "totally fulfilled." Yet his patient face and his sincere blue eyes pierce my soul. I've got to hand it to him—he definitely has something I don't have, and somehow I'm totally buying it. If ever I've met someone who seems totally at peace in his heart, mind, and soul, Jim Downing is that man.

"I want that," I say. And then I look around the table at the other men and ask, with a note of incredulity, "Who doesn't want that, right?"

I'm not looking for reassurance from my husband and Jim's son, but honestly—I mean, really—*who doesn't want to be totally fulfilled? Isn't it the holy grail?*

Jim smiles and chuckles softly, a sound I will soon come to recognize as his joyful, knowing way of saying, *Wait until you see the great thing I am about to show you.*

"Well, Dianne," Jim says, "I'd like to study the Bible with you. Would you like to do that?"

"Sure," I reply, surprising even myself with my instant answer. I can't seem to help myself; I'm compelled. I want to understand more about how he found this peace, how he became so satisfied, so fulfilled. I can tell that this wholeness comes from something far more profound than just a long life. I want to know the secrets of his wisdom.

"How do we do that?" I ask.

"Let's meet back here this Tuesday morning. Just bring your Bible, and we will go from there."

He drops these casual details about Bibles and meetings on Tuesdays. I find myself pulled in—hook, line, and sinker. I can't believe it, but we don't even talk about Pearl Harbor, the very thing I thought I would learn more about. It's only an introductory lunch, filled with small talk and one giant bomb of a question.

We wrap up our lunch with plans for the next one. Pete and I say our goodbyes to Jim and his son, and we walk silently to the car. We don't say much on the way back home.

I think to myself, over and over, *What on earth did I just sign up for?*

I was raised Catholic. I grew up in a congregation where we didn't do this Bible-reading business.

We touch the holy water as we enter church, listen to the homily, and make the sign of the cross a million times. We get Communion, we sit-stand-kneel several times, and then we head out to return to our lives forty-five minutes later.

But a Bible? Of my own? No, I have no clue where mine might be. Wherever it's hiding, I know for sure it's still wrapped in the cellophane it came in when I was confirmed in the Catholic church just before I married

Pete. I'm embarrassed to say this, but I don't think I ever opened it.

Well, just in case you're in the market for a Bible and want to subtly slip into Barnes & Noble to purchase one, let me warn you: The Bible shelves are not on display in a quiet, private place. Nope—they are RIGHT IN FRONT OF THE TABLES AT THE COFFEE SHOP. I'm annoyed and horrified. This is just too exposed. I start sweating. I feel like everyone can see how little I know, what a heathen I am—like everyone in the store is watching me, judging me: The new TV lady is shopping for a Bible!

I pull out my phone and do a quick Google search: "top-rated study Bible." A quick skim of reviews says the ESV is easy to read and has notes on the bottom of the page that explain what is really happening—great. Yes, I'll take it. I grab the thick white paperback, hurry to the counter to pay, and rush out to the safety and anonymity of my car.

What have I gotten myself into? I think. *Fine. I have a Bible now. But I truly can't take those "religy" types, so please don't let this be some experience where the Bible is beaten into me.*

Just like me and long drives . . . I simply won't make it.

CHAPTER 3

TUESDAY PEOPLE

Lunch and a Lesson

I SOON LEARN that the table in the Garden of the Gods Club—the one near the fireplace—is Jim's special spot, the sacred space where he meets with his most trusted advisers and closest friends.

"Mr. Downing, how nice it is to see you." Each staff member greets Jim by name as they approach his table, refilling our water glasses. We hear about the menu specials, even though they know he will only, ever, always have a cup of soup with oyster crackers.

"And how lovely it is to see you," he answers in reply. Jim knows each one's name and asks about their children, their families, and their lives outside of work. He takes a personal interest in everyone, and there seems to be a constant stream of people passing by his table. Everyone wants a chance to say hello and to meet his newest guest. Jim's warm, blue eyes hold the wisdom of a lifetime as he makes space for each person— including me.

When our lunches come—a basket of muffins, my salad, and always Jim's cup of soup, I uncap my pen and open my notebook, ready to write down everything he says. This new adventure feels a lot like the beginning of a new semester at school, and—I don't mind telling you—I am so good at school.

I am not the kind of person who will stroll the aisle of office supplies and buy pens of every color, but I have a handful of pens at the bottom of my purse, sprinkled with face powder and smeared with wayward lip gloss. The Bible is my brand-new textbook, and all I need is a clearly outlined syllabus.

With my pen poised over the page, I probably look like a bright-eyed cocker spaniel at obedience school, alert and eager to please. "So, where do we begin?"

His smile is sly as he taps his finger on the cover of his Bible. "Dianne, the answers to all of your questions are right here."

Our Bibles sit side by side on the white tablecloth.

My Bible looks fresh and crisp, right off the bookstore shelf; I haven't even cracked the spine all the way. Jim's Bible looks used and tattered; the gold leafing has worn off the pages, and the leather cover has softened from decades of page-turning.

"My friend," he says, "once upon a time, there was a prophet named Jeremiah. He wrote these words: 'When I discovered your words, I devoured them. They are my joy and my heart's delight, for I bear your name, O LORD God of Heaven's Armies.'"[1]

"Devoured?"

"Devoured. Gobbled them up, like a delicious feast. I'd like to teach you a method for personal Bible study, a step-by-step process that will allow you to know Christ, devour the contents of this book, and find the answers you need."

This seems impossible to me. As a journalist, I spend my days digging for information, and there's no way I can imagine that the answers to some major life questions are simply waiting in this book in front of me. It can't be that easy, that accessible. I smile like I understand, but inside I feel like I'm too much of a heathen to really get good at any of this.

"Each week, I will give you a passage to study, and we will use what I call the ABC method. Before you do any reading or writing at all, you're going to pray."

I nod—like, of course, this is what I always do before I read anything at all.

"Invite the Holy Spirit into this space with you, and ask God to show you what he wants you to see today. Then I want you to read the chosen passage three times. You can read silently if you'd like, but sometimes it's also helpful to read it out loud at least once. Read nice and slow, pausing at the end of each verse to reflect on what you've just read."

Read three times. So far, so good.

"After you've read the passage, the first step is to create a title for the chapter you're reading. Chapters of the Bible are often broken down into smaller sections with their own subheadings, and you can use these to help you, but you'll remember it more if you create your own title for the chapter."

I take notes. **A:** After reading the passage, create a title for the chapter.

"I imagine you're very good at titles, being a journalist and all." He leaned in. "Jot down two or three titles that come to mind, and then choose one that is as fitting and complete as possible."

"Yep. Got it. Complete and fitting. A tight sound bite."

"Then, **B**, choose the best verse. One of the verses will jump out at you. It will grab your heart and get your attention. That's the best one."

I nod—he's speaking my newsroom language. "So this may be the only easy part of this process for me. I do this every day at work, and I teach new journalists how to do it: Search for the most compelling part of the story—the lede—and open with that."

"Agreed," Jim says. "Find the most important part."

"Sometimes in the newsroom we tease each other for burying the lede. I'm always like, 'You saved the best part for the end of the story? What if your viewers don't make it that far because you didn't pull them in quickly?' Our goal is to keep viewers, not lose them in the first five seconds by not grabbing their attention."

"Yes, just like in the newsroom, Dianne—find the most compelling part. You can trust me on this, and you can trust God to show you. That's why you pray before you begin, to ask him to show you."

He smiles again, flashing that twinkle in his eye. Jim communicates so much with his smile and his eyes because the rest of his body is mostly always still. I am trained to be so aware of my body movements on the air, and sitting next to him, I feel fidgety and busy if I move at all. The man is so present, so engaged. Maybe he is comfortable in his own skin, or maybe this is how the body changes after ninety-nine years. Maybe he is just done moving if he doesn't have to.

He makes the smallest movement with his hand,

the only part of himself he gestures with, and he says, "Then, C, pick your most challenging verse. There will be something in that passage that challenges you, pushes you to question something in your life."

"Challenge me . . . how?" I ask.

"Well, maybe there's something you need to stop doing, or start doing, a new habit you need to put into place. Maybe it's a new truth that you need to weave into your life."

I look down at my list of instructions. I'm supposed to do this with the whole Bible? "This step seems like it could take a while, Jim."

"And it sure could. Everything that's good takes time. Remember, Dianne, we want to devour this Scripture. You don't want to just smell that salad in front of you, do you?"

"No, Jim, I'm going to eat it." I laugh, putting lettuce and other veggies onto my fork and into my mouth. I'm being polite with my salad since Jim has only his cup of soup, but let me tell you—I could put down a cheese-burger and fries every night of the week. There's nothing I don't like to eat. I'm basically a garbage disposal. I can outeat any of my friends.

When my mouth is empty again, I say, "*Devour* is a word I can wrap my mind around."

"That's right. You need all the nutrients you can find."

"So do I write down a challenge, like I would a goal?" *Goals and checklists*, I think. *Just tell me what to do, Professor, and I'll make my way down the list.*

"You could do that, yes," he says. "Write down the truth you have found, and then write down how it applies to you, what it might reveal about who you are and who you want to become. Make it personal to you, Dianne, and then decide what you plan to do about it."

"So it's a long-term project?" I ask, trying not to show my hesitation.

I don't like long-term projects, Jim, I think.

I like to move fast, get to the heart of the story, and move on. I analyze so many facts all day long . . . I'm not sure how I could settle in with one sentence or one section of the Bible, reading and rereading it to find the challenge, without losing interest completely.

"No, think of it more as a weekly assignment," he says. "Give yourself a task you can do this very week, something tangible and practical. Because remember, next week you'll have a new passage, and that will bring a new challenge for you to work on. So choose a small way you can take action right away."

"Can you give me an example, please?" I ask. I don't

mean to sound needy or like I don't understand, but I really like to get things right the first time.

"Oh, like asking forgiveness, or apologizing to someone, or memorizing a verse," Jim says.

Oh, boy. Apologies and forgiveness . . .

I keep my face down even as I write down those weighted words. They are . . . a little too much to take in right now. I'll have to think about them later.

Maybe. Maybe not.

But the other concern must register on my face. *Memorizing? What? I don't want to memorize anything! What's the point in that when we have Google?*

I trust this man in front of me, for reasons I can't even explain. He's lived decades longer than most people, and he exudes a hard-won wisdom of so many years. I know his faith is deep. I know he has insights that I want. I've decided to believe what he is telling me . . . but memorize? Ew.

It's like he's read my mind. "Don't worry, Dianne. We'll start small, with just one or two verses a week."

I should hope so, I think. *That's the only way I can be successful in this master class.*

I say, "Jim, can I be honest, though? I used to memorize a lot of things, and I guess I think I know how, but that's not how I learn best. I just feel like I'm, well . . .

memorizing it. But it's not going to stick with me. I'm not really internalizing it."

"But you see, Dianne, internalizing is *exactly* what you're doing when you memorize."

No. I do not see, I think.

He must understand what I'm thinking, because he smiles again and begins to explain that when you memorize a verse, it becomes part of you. It returns to you when nothing else will. It takes root in your soul. "Memorizing," he says again, "*is* internalizing."

I sigh, realizing this is going to be a thing. I've already committed to do what he says on this path to fulfillment, so I guess I'm into memorizing now.

"Then, **D** is for **difficult**," Jim says, moving right along. "As you read, you might come across something unfamiliar, a concept that's hard to wrap your mind around, something you don't feel you can explain, or maybe something that just doesn't make sense."

"I think that might be a lot of it, Jim," I whisper.

Immediately I'm having flashbacks to my religion class in my Catholic high school, when one teacher gave each student a brown scapular—two pieces of wool strung together and blessed by a priest; we wore it under our uniforms, believing we were wearing a fabric associated with the Virgin Mary. The teacher insisted we must wear our brown scapular all day, every day. I didn't really understand what it was, but he said if we died without wearing it, we wouldn't get into heaven. That's a heavy burden to carry in two pieces of wool! It made no sense to me then, even though wise people insisted it was true.

What if the Bible is full of things like this, I wondered— *random laws that seem out of touch and irrelevant? The list of "difficult things" could be long.*

Again, Jim speaks as if he could read my thoughts. "We will deal with each one of those difficult things, Dianne. Don't just decide that you can't understand them; write down specifically what is difficult for you. Then we can talk about it together."

"Okay," I say, nodding and raising my eyebrows. Days ago I had wondered what I'd signed up for . . . and now I wonder whether Jim knows what *he* signed up for, giving me permission to ask all my questions.

"Finally, write a summary of the passage," he says.

"Summary . . ." I look down at my list: *A, B, C, D . . . S*. "Jim, it seems like it should start with an *E*."

He laughs. "Then we can call it . . . the essentials. Write down the essentials of what you just read."

My face lights up again with recognition. How I love when he talks me through steps I can relate to by summarizing the essentials. I tell him, "It's like when a reporter pitches a story to the newsroom, telling us the best and most important parts. They summarize what we really need to know; the short, twenty-second version of a story that may have unfolded over several days. *Essentials*. Got it."

"Exactly. A paragraph or two."

"Wait, Jim, did you say paragraphs? In the newsroom, a summary can be as few as three words. It's called a 'slug,' actually. It's three words long, like 'Crash on I-25' or 'Fire at School.'"

"Sure, those work," he says. "You'll probably want more than three words, but aim for that twenty-second story you like."

I smile. "Jim, you're speaking my language. So what's next?"

He reaches for his Bible and flips it open about two-thirds through. "I'm awfully fond of the Gospel of John," he says. "Many people have found Jesus by reading that book alone, and it's a great place to begin your study. Let's start there."

I feel like such a novice. I copy his actions, opening my Bible about two-thirds of the way through. The spine cracks and creaks with the newness of laying open. I thumb through the corners until I find it, hoping I'll land on the right page. I'm faking it, completely.

He reads aloud to me. "For God so loved the world

that he gave his one and only Son, that whoever believes in him shall not perish but have eternal life."[2]

I hear his words: *Whoever believes in him shall not perish.*

Gosh, I want to get this right so badly from Assignment One, but this verse is already difficult for me. *Perish?* Wait, what? So everyone who doesn't believe will perish? I know plenty of peaceful, loving people who follow other religions, and I can't imagine that they won't be in heaven just because they believe differently. I hate to start out by disagreeing, but this is going to be very hard for me.

"Jim, how can you say everyone else will perish?" I ask. "How can you say that?"

"Well, I didn't say it," he answers. "John did. He was teaching the Good News of Jesus Christ, that anyone who believes in him can have eternal life." Jim says these words with the certainty of the sound of a judge's gavel pounding.

"But Jim, I know so many people who have been taught different things, have lived inside different faith lifestyles, and I can't just write them off. How can we say that they're not going to heaven? They're good people. Kind people."

His voice is gentle. He says, "But being good and kind is not the way to heaven. We can't get there by the things we do. It's about our belief, our faith in Jesus Christ. He didn't die only for the good and kind people. He died for everyone. *Everyone*. And when we each accept this truth, accept his grace for all the things we get wrong, and agree that he is the way to eternal life, then we open our hands to receive the gift he has given us."

Nobody has ever explained it to me this way before, and I don't understand how he can be so sure. It's too much for me. I'm picturing the faces of people I know—people I love—who believe different things. They are just as sure of their truth as Jim is of his own. How can they both be right? I have so many questions, and I have so much to learn, and it doesn't feel very good.

He says, "Well done, Dianne. You're already asking the hard questions."

Even as I feel the discomfort of disagreeing, I feel like I have somehow stumbled into sacred space. Yes, my feelings about God and the Bible are uncertain and unresolved, but I know instinctively that this is special—a one-on-one Bible study with someone who has devoted eight decades to the pursuit. So many others are asking for appointments on his schedule; why do I get the honor of his time? And how can I do this when I really have no clue about the Bible?

And so Jim and I begin our Tuesdays together. Each

week he gives me the same list of tasks for my assignment, and each week I go home to grapple with a new passage. I question everything. *Am I getting it? Can he see how much I don't know? Does it seem like I'm faking interest?* I mean, I'm not faking anything. I am deeply interested, so I keep after it, waiting for this path to fulfillment he promised me. I don't feel it, I have to be honest. But I decide to trust the process. There is something so simple and yet comforting about opening the Bible, and I want to believe answers can be found.

Every time we meet, we discuss my notes, my challenges, my difficulties, and my summaries. And let me tell you, if Jim picks the same key verses from the passage, I feel like a third grader who got a gold star on a homework assignment. His words are affirmation in a world where I feel cautiously optimistic. He sure seems to believe I can do this, but I still don't trust myself to know what I'm doing, or even to be sure of what "this" is.

We become Tuesday people, as Jim and I meet week after week. And you know, now that I think about it, he never even touched his cup of soup. I guess he had other things to devour.

CHAPTER 4

A PIECE OF THE STORY

Jim and Pearl Harbor

A FRIEND ONCE TOLD ME that one of the best things I can do for my professional life is to write handwritten notes. Rather than sending emails and texts, I write notes using an actual pen on actual paper. That practice has served me very well. I love a good handwritten note.

But Jim Downing took the handwritten note to a whole new level.

Jim was a gunner's mate first class and the postmaster onboard the USS *West Virginia* in 1941. It was his job to deliver love letters from wives, updates from children, and care packages from parents to the men onboard the ship. He got to go home every night to his young bride, Morena—they were newlyweds, married only a few months—and they often hosted men for breakfast on the weekend. The day he tells me about Pearl Harbor,[1] he tells me first about those mornings, about his wife in her apron, serving up bacon and eggs to hungry men who loved a good, hearty breakfast.

Their home was in Honolulu, on Oahu's south shore, about twenty minutes from the harbor. On the morning of December 7, 1941, Jim and his companions heard a distant explosion, and then suddenly the alarmingly nearby shriek of an incoming shell racing over the roof and crashing into his backyard.

One of the men turned on the radio in the corner of the room to hear the broadcaster say, "I have phoned army and navy intelligence, and they have advised us that the island of Oahu is under enemy attack. The enemy has not been identified. Stay tuned. We will give more information when we get it."

Something was very wrong.

The other men were in uniform, but, Jim says, he was wearing a Hawaiian shirt. He tore into their bedroom to change into his uniform so he could follow the sounds and the smoke with the others.

When he came out of the bedroom, he heard the latest update: "Pearl Harbor is under enemy attack.

The enemy has been identified as Japan. All servicemen return to your ship or station."

Just before Jim joined two other sailors in his friend Herb's car to go to the harbor, he turned to face Morena, for maybe the very last time. He kissed her face, and as he jumped into the car, she shouted, "Deuteronomy 33:27! 'The eternal God is your refuge, and underneath are the everlasting arms.'" As his car pulled away, he saw the tears in her eyes. She was, he tells me, still wearing her apron from fixing breakfast.

What a woman. I picture myself in that same situation, an inferno of flames, shrieks, planes, explosives, and complete chaos. I would have grabbed my husband and begged him not to go, but Morena was selfless and courageous, commissioning him to go. Goodness. The closest I have come are at the many deployment ceremonies I've covered for the news, when I watch these families say goodbye to their troops, with no promise or certainty that they'll see them again. Military families are a wonder to me. An absolute wonder.

The car raced through the neighborhood streets of Oahu, and it took Jim and his friends much longer than the usual twenty minutes to get to their stations, since roads were now packed with other cars filled with men on the same mission.

Jim describes what the scene looked like as he and

his friends arrived within view of Battleship Row. Japanese planes zigzagged the sky, diving at the harbor. There was devastation and horror all around, and everything above the waterline was on fire. One ship was upside down, another was spewing smoke like a volcano. Jim's ship, the USS *West Virginia*, was sinking and on fire. Oil had spilled from holes in the damaged ships, and the water was on fire. The men who had jumped or been thrown from their vessels were burning alive.

Jim knew immediately that many of his friends were already dead.

As he was trying to get near his ship, a Japanese plane flew so low that Jim threw his body to the ground just as the machine gunfire opened on him and his group. He tells me that the experience was burned into his memory: the pulsing in his ears, even the image of the pilot's face. The plane was so near to the ground that Jim could see the pilot's goggles and the whites of his eyes and his teeth.

Jim picked himself up off the ground, determined to get to his ship. He climbed onto the nearest vessel, the USS *Tennessee*, knowing that his ship was just on the other side of the opposite railing. It was too far to jump, but the barrel of a gun stretched across the water and just over the railing of the USS *West Virginia*. So

Jim climbed up and over, before sliding down onto the deck of his ship.

He found himself aboard a nearly abandoned vessel that had lost all power. The fire had spread from the bow to the middle, and the flames were already upon the lockers that stored the ammunition. Without power, he couldn't fight back—he could only fight to protect what was left.

Jim grabbed a fire hose that stretched over from the USS *Tennessee* and sprayed down the flames that were threatening the ammunition lockers. The ship was covered in yards of thick, flammable paint that would make a great fire. He tells me that he knew he was battling a ticking bomb: "I knew, *I've got to put out the fire so there won't be a secondary explosion. Or this will be the end.*"

He saw one body after another, crewmen lying on the deck—men with stories, with families and friends. Jim walked down the deck, spraying water toward the flames, and memorized the names of his comrades. It was a small and painful offering, to be able to give closure to the people who loved these men, but Jim was determined. When he could not identify their faces because of the burns, he searched for their dog tags.

Japanese fighter planes continued to attack. Jim manned the fire hose and prayed, "I'll see you in a minute, Jesus."

Jim believed he would be killed, and he wasn't afraid of the end. For more than a half hour, he battled the flames, memorizing the names of his friends and expecting to meet God at any moment—and feeling completely at peace.

A second wave of Japanese attacks struck the harbor, and the ships continued to take fire from the enemy until finally it was over. The USS *West Virginia* sank under the weight of the damage.

Jim describes to me the emergency burn unit outside the navy hospital, where he visited a friend that afternoon. Many of the men were blind from the explosions, and their hair had burned off. He says he went down the line and spoke with each soldier, some of them blinded and others wounded in other debilitating ways, and he told them, "If you dictate a note, I'll see that your parents get it."

I stare at him in awe and ask, "Jim, what did they say to their parents? What does a person say in those moments?"

"Well, these guys stayed optimistic, assuring their families there was nothing to worry about. They told me to write things like 'Don't worry about me; I'll be alright,' even though they knew they wouldn't make it through the night."

I know he doesn't like to hear it, but I just have to say it. "Jim, you are a true hero."

He replies, "I felt proud of the way that our men responded so valiantly—unarmed and without leadership. I was so thankful to them, for them. Everybody was a hero that day."

He's quiet a moment, then says, "It wasn't difficult for me to write those letters to their parents—each one took only a few minutes."

I remember that Jim had also taken the time to memorize the names of his dead crewmates that very morning, when under attack. At a critical juncture when he could have defended himself, when all evidence appeared he was moments away from his own death, he showed total kindness to others. He focused all his efforts on saving the ship but also honored each individual who had just given their life.

I realize now why I have trusted Jim from the moment I met him. He is the embodiment of integrity, honor, and kindness. He's everything I aim to become.

CHAPTER 5

IN THE FISHBOWL

Affirmation and Meditation

NOTHING I WRITE could ever follow Jim's story appropriately. Nothing. There is no way to transition from the magnitude of his service to the minutiae of what I'm about to tell you. But I have more to tell you, more I learned from this man whose life transcends my brief story with him. And to get to the next important thing he taught me, I have to make a confession:

I have a codependent relationship with my snooze button.

I love it and I hate it. I need it and I despise it. I set the alarm because I have to get up, and I press the snooze button because I cannot bear to get up yet. The thought of jumping out of bed from a dead sleep—how do people do that? Who are those people? I press snooze at least once, often as many as five times, as if another ten minutes will be the restoration of my soul. It is a false sense of control, but it is apparently one I need. See? Codependent.

My mind doesn't rest, even when I am sleeping. I often dream about tornadoes, which I read means that I am overwhelmed, spinning with thoughts, and worried about dangers that may never affect me. My mind is a constant loop of conversations, reminders, busyness, and playing catch-up. Constant.

When I finally decide I've hit the snooze enough times, the first two coherent minutes go something like this:

I grab my phone immediately to find out what I have missed overnight. All of that "sleep" might have caused me to miss something "important." I put it in quotes, not because it's not important but because in the newsroom, *everything is*. Self-care is secondary to the news. I wake up feeling behind.

I scroll through the headlines on the news, and then I skim a family group text, followed by a dozen messages that arrived overnight from two of my best girlfriends and another text from Barrett—the funniest guy I know, who makes me laugh until I cry. I want to check in with everybody, and I haven't even poured my coffee yet.

I stagger to the kitchen with my bleary eyes still on the phone. The coffee maker pulls me, when what I really want is mostly the sweetness of my creamer in a warm mug. I pour myself the coffee, adding cream until it's far closer to a latte than an espresso. I multitask, still scrolling through apps on my phone, checking headlines, stats, the weather, and Facebook updates.

Then I see it: a rogue comment from an internet troll. "You are disgusting. You have no business being on the air broadcasting the news."

Internet trolls are the perpetual bullies on the playground of life, and they are relentless. They are bottom-feeders, fueled by toxins and vitriol, and they follow me into my kitchen. They pour into my psyche like poison into my morning coffee.

When I became a journalist, I thought I understood the weighty magnitude of opinions, the approval and disapproval of so many people who watched me and thought they knew me. I didn't imagine it would be easy, but I actually thought that—maybe, just maybe—I could bear it. I thought I could tolerate it. I thought maybe I could survive the gauntlet without being torn to shreds.

Well, more than twenty years later, it's now clear to me: I can't. The truth is that nobody can.

Some hardened individuals might pretend like a barrage of scathing comments don't hurt, and I would love to know their secret. When you know what the burn feels like, you can recognize somebody else who's trying not to melt.

I often feel like I'm in a fishbowl of observation. Readers, viewers, and internet trolls scrutinize my life in ways that can feel degrading and dehumanizing. I used to console myself by believing they only felt powerful behind their screen names, that their anonymity gave them the permission to say things on a screen that they'd never truly say face-to-face. But then my public profile grew, I became more visible in my everyday life, and I started meeting people who actually said those degrading, dehumanizing things directly to my face.

No place is guarded enough. At the doctor's office, literally before my name is called to enter the exam room, a viewer will stop me to tell me how I should cover different kinds of stories. People will interrupt me on a rare date night with my husband, a once in a blue moon occasion when the stars have aligned and our work schedules are free, to ask why I haven't given more airtime to their preferred candidate in an election. Someone will stop me when I'm in the grocery store and insist that now is the time to give me feedback on my haircut. I try to slip away by offering my business card and an invitation to email me, but the person will prattle on about something she doesn't like about me, and I will spend twenty minutes navigating the dynamics of her opinion and my envy of other people who get to choose their produce in peace.

Oh, how I wish there were a class called Emotional Intelligence 101. The syllabus could include topics like "The Things You Should Not Say," "The Moments You Should Not Interrupt," and "The Great Should-Nots of Human Interaction."

Here's the first thing I'd say if I were to teach that class: Unless I place a microphone in front of you, I'm probably not interested in your opinion.

I've spent years—and a lot of hours in professional therapy—working on boundaries and an exit strategy from those conversations. But I feel like I have to listen, grinning and bearing it, giving the viewer a voice. I stay in the conversation because I've been trained that "you don't want them to say you're rude." I stand still in the produce section and keep the smile on my face because I am one of the faces of our news station, and this core value is stitched into me: *Dianne, we need for them to like you.*

I don't even know what it means or looks like for

them to like me. Do they "like" me because my appearance that day appeals to them? Do they "like" me because I show visible compassion to the mom who lost her baby in a car accident? Do they "like" me because I go after government officials they don't like? Do they "like" me because I attended their event to raise money for their charity?

And what do I do when someone feels the freedom to say something mean? Am I supposed to just ignore that? To make it not hurt? Give me a break. It hurts.

Mostly it just shocks me, even after all these years in this career. When I see hurtful messages from viewers, first I want to cry. Then I want to fight back. Then I send a screenshot to my best friend, who crafts a reply I'll never send, words that soothe my heart and leave me laughing. Because the truth is, I can't fight for myself in this sphere. I never do, because they "have to like me." So I usually try to numb the pain with the art of distraction, scrolling through more headlines while the cup of coffee turns lukewarm in my hands.

If it's a Tuesday morning, then I know I have to get moving. I have a meeting with Jim—who is always on time. I start reminding myself, BE ON TIME TODAY, DIANNE. I believe tardiness sends the message that your time is more valuable than the other person's. Don't be late.

And then the self-doubts creep in over why I should have the privilege of his time at all. What if I interpreted my Bible study all wrong? What if today is the day he discovers I'm more heathen than holy, more distracted than disciplined? What if I don't earn any gold stars at the top of my paper?

I feel hungry, but having a leisurely breakfast at home might make me late, so I should probably eat in the car. I get my act together and get myself out the door, nearly late, despite my good intentions and best efforts.

After many meetings at the Garden of the Gods Club, Jim invites me to meet at his home. Things have become so comfortable between us—warm greetings and deep conversations. He says that sometimes it feels like I'm his adopted granddaughter, so I start calling him Grandpa Jim.

I'm always hurrying when I arrive at his front door, and I have to be careful because he's often waiting for me in his wheelchair, just inside the door. Classic me, in a hurry. Classic Jim, ready and waiting.

Jim's smile welcomes me as I walk in. "So good to see you, Dianne."

I lean down to his wheelchair to hug him. "Hi, Grandpa Jim. How are you?"

"I'm wonderful. So happy you're here, Dianne. You are the bright spot in my day!"

He probably says this to each person who comes into his home, but I receive this compliment as if it were a bouquet of wildflowers he has chosen just for me.

I follow him to his sitting room, the hallway lined with marks from his motorized wheelchair, appropriately nicknamed "The Destroyer." (You'd call it that, too, if you were to feel its crushing force rolling over your feet.) He navigates The Destroyer like a bumper car in his office, nudging tables and chairs as it beeps with forward and reverse circles until he's satisfied and positioned where he wants to be.

We are surrounded by papers, plants, Bibles, and so many books. People give him books all the time, and he receives them all like a perpetual reading list, as if he still had so much more to learn about life. The books are piled high around the sitting area. I glance at his new titles and say, "Jim, your library is constantly expanding. Look at these."

"It's more than I can read in a lifetime. I'll never get through them all." He chuckles and gestures to his library. "Take any of them that you'd like."

His room is always warm, sometimes intolerably so. The sunshine falls onto the chair where I am sitting, making the air even warmer, probably seventy-five or eighty degrees. I draw the curtain closed behind me to give me a little shade.

Carol, his caretaker, keeps the room warm because Jim is always cold. She arrives soon with her famous spiced iced tea, with fresh herbs and an orange slice on the rim. It's the most delicious thing in a cup.

There's one thing very oddly out of place in his room: a plastic replica of the bloody stump of an arm. It's just hanging out up there on the bookshelf. If that's odd to read on the page right now, imagine how I felt looking at this prank prop in the stately room of this dignified man.

Jim is a lover of practical jokes, and this is his favorite one. He once told me, "When I speak to university students, they see this old man take the stage, and I know they probably think I'm old and tired, without much left to give. So I arrange to have this arm inside the sleeve of my coat, and I ask to have someone come and help move me. They come up, they reach for what they think is both of my hands, they pull on the arm, and this bloody stump comes out."

I've never seen this in person, but every time Jim retells the story, his eyes twinkle even brighter. He loves to hear the audience collectively gasp when the plastic bloody stump slides out of his sleeve, right into someone's hand. My friend and mentor is not nearly as fragile as the youngsters might imagine. "I guess you could say it's an icebreaker," he says.

And so Grandpa Jim and I settle in for our weekly conversation. The next hour and a half always transforms my spirit from a spinning tornado to a calm breeze. Always. For ninety minutes of each week, I am calm. This small window of time is the eye of my storm.

We talk about the verse or passage he assigned for me to study, and then Jim moves on to a new lesson, something he wants me to know. "Dianne, I thought that today we could start by defining meditation."

He's not trying to be funny, so I catch myself before I laugh out loud at the timing of it all. He likely doesn't know the irony—how I am rushed, and now he wants to teach me about stillness.

He is never, ever in a hurry. Even when I'm scrambling for answers, he gives them to me in a slow stream, sometimes so slow that I interrupt him with my own answers again. I know some things about meditation, because I have practiced yoga for years, but Jim is talking about something else. I can tell.

If I sit still, I have to be with my own thoughts, my truths, or the lingering comments from critics. Those are not always my favorite companions, so I crowd my life with busyness. My mind races with thoughts that bounce like a ball inside a pinball machine, and I have become comfortable with the noise.

"Jim, I don't like to sit still. I can't even do long car

rides without falling asleep. If Pete isn't interested in talking in the car, well then, nighty night. I'm out. I can't imagine thinking about nothing."

Jim gives me a measured look, like he wonders how I can live without space for quiet. "Well, thinking about nothing isn't necessarily meditation," he says. "It's not the same as being still. When do you think your thoughts? How do you determine what's going on in your heart? How do you know what you really want and need?"

I wince. He's right. I have long wanted to get a tattoo on my wrist that says "Be Still," but I never have. It's just not me . . . and I'm not sure whether I mean the phrase or the tattoo. The idea of a tattoo on my skin immediately invokes thoughts of judgment. Will I get in trouble with my boss? What will my viewers think, that I am some sort of free-thinking rebel with time to be still? I cannot imagine that kind of freedom, to get permanent ink on my skin, a permanent reminder of a daily goal. Nope. *So* not me.

I tell Jim about this almost-tattoo, and he says, "It sounds like you care very much about what other people think of you. What is that like for you?" His tone is so gentle that I try not to cry at the compassion in his voice.

I feel tension in my shoulders at the suggestion of the weight of it all. "I'm tired, Jim."

He asks, "How do you handle the weight of all this criticism? What do the people in your line of work suggest?"

I sigh, thinking of the empty answers I've heard. "Well, they'll tell me it's part of the job, saying, 'You signed up for this' or 'Get thicker skin'—or my personal favorite, 'Dianne, you have to learn to stop being so sensitive.' I don't even know how to do that—how does one unlearn who they are?"

"So they're telling you to stop being you?" he replies. "Why would you want to do that?"

I don't want to do that. But I feel like I have to measure their opinions.

"I'm thinking about one of Aesop's fables," he says thoughtfully. "This Greek man had a donkey he wanted to sell, so he took his son and the donkey and headed to market. At the first village they came to, the people said, 'You're foolish because you should be riding, not walking.' So the man put his son on the donkey. At the next village, the people criticized the young man for riding while his father was walking. So the father got on the donkey. At the next village, the people criticized him for overloading the donkey. So they tied his feet together and put a pole in between his feet, and they tried to carry the donkey on the pole. The donkey squirmed out of their ropes, fell off the bridge, and drowned in the river. So the man and his son had to go home without the donkey. When you try to please everybody, you please nobody." His eyes twinkle again as he adds, "And you may lose your donkey in the process."

After another moment, he speaks more directly. "Dianne, you cannot worry about what other people say. Jesus' opinion is the only one that matters."

I sit there while his words hang in the air. He lets me feel uncomfortable with what he just said. "So you're saying no opinions matter? Not even my family's or my spouse's?" I ask.

"Not even them," he says, shaking his head. "If you are doing what is right in the eyes of God, why should anyone else matter?" He smiles slightly. "It's the most fun to be yourself."

For once in my life, I have no words. My rapid-fire questions cease. I need to just sit with this for a minute. I can embrace this in my personal life, but in the newsroom? How could I even convince one person on my team that the opinion of Jesus is the only one that matters? It's laughable. I don't want to be disrespectful, but this conversation is a nonstarter with TV executives.

After what feels like ten minutes of silence, I realize the next question I have, then ask him, "Jim, how do you never get angry?"

"What makes you think I never get angry?"

"Um, I've never seen it. I can't even picture it, Jim."

"Well, anyone who travels with me will tell you I have my limits. I get angry when my flights are delayed, making me late to see someone."

Even then, I don't picture him throwing a fit in the airport. There's no way he gets as angry as I feel. It's not even within his capacity.

Jim says, "The origin of anger is selfishness. It's based on a feeling that says, 'I want what I want when I want it.' The anger turns into frustration, and frustration can turn into violence. Taking my anger out on someone will do nothing to ease the pain in my heart." He pushes me to consider the consequences. "What good would it do?"

He raises a strong question. I don't have an answer. I ask, "So, what do you do with the anger? How do you deal with the hurt, Jim?"

He smiles. "That brings us nicely back to today's topic: meditation. I was speaking to a group of congressional summer aides about meditation one night. They had the same look on their faces that you have right now on yours. But this one trainee there began to squirm. He held up his hand, and I knew he had something he had to say. He told us that he had just finished a $40,000 research study for his congressman, and the subject was what factors set the tone for the day. They had discovered that you have a measure of control over whether you're going to have a good or bad day."

I'm nodding and leaning forward. "Tell me, Jim."

"They discovered it all comes down to how you spend the last few minutes before you go to bed and how you spend the first few minutes after you get up. It's about focusing your thoughts . . . meditation."

I laugh, thinking of my first five minutes of the morning. My first five minutes of *any morning*.

"I certainly don't spend my first five minutes like that. I'm the Snooze Button Queen. I wait until the very last second to get up. I am not calm, and I am always rushed. I mean, I don't love it, no. I want to change it, but for a mind as busy as mine? When the alarm goes off and I have to choose between more sleep and waking up so I can sit still and be quiet . . . I'm going to hit the alarm clock just one more time."

He smiles. "I'd like for you to try it. Meditate on the right thing a few minutes before you go to bed and a few minutes before you start the day."

I honestly cannot see myself doing this.

"Choose something meaningful to think on. Something that is true, good, and lovely. A synonym for meditation has to do with the animal world—that phrase *chewing the cud*. A dairy cow swallows her grass or hay whole, then lies down in the shade to regurgitate and chew on it. Meditation is chewing on something to get the nourishment out of it."

(That's an odd analogy, but I can see where he's going with it.)

"You want to choose something good and optimistic. There is a Bible verse that says, 'As a man thinks in his heart, so he is.'[1] We become what we are meditating on. It should be something that brings God into the picture in your mind. I've found the book of Psalms and the book of Proverbs in the Bible are the very best for this."

"You do this every day?"

"Every day. And I find that when people say they don't have time . . . well, those are the people who need it most."

Like me.

I can't see myself getting good at this.

But I can't dismiss what he's saying, because one thing I've learned from the hundreds of people I've interviewed in my career is that the happiest are the ones who know God. I've interviewed people who have great wealth and people who live in deep, deep poverty. I've been in the home of a billionaire, the most opulent home I've ever seen . . . but the heaviness was so present. Joy doesn't live there. But again and again, I discover that the people I meet who are most content have faith; they are centered in peace that can only be found by having a connection with something higher, someone bigger than them.

He puts his hand on mine. "Dianne, as long as you are pleasing Jesus, no one's opinion matters but his. The truth is, he loves and forgives you, no matter what. When viewers won't give you another chance, remember Jesus is the God of a million chances."

I place my hand on his. "Jim, I'm going to need all the second chances I can get."

CHAPTER 6

ONE HUNDRED YEARS

The Power of Looking Forward

IT'S FUN TO SHOW hundredth-birthday celebrations on our newscasts. The parties are typically held at nursing homes and are usually accompanied by cake, balloons, and past photos of the centenarians. As we edit the videos, we zoom in on the smiles on their faces—everyone wants to see what "one hundred years old" looks like. We then share short segments from the interviews and end with their secrets of longevity. They're always so simple: Don't sweat the small stuff, enjoy each day to the fullest, count your blessings. Most of us just make life complicated, but people who have lived for so long have got it figured out.

Jim teases me that his secret to longevity is in choosing good grandparents, as if it's all in the genes. But all joking aside, Jim's answer always comes down to the truth: A fruitful life consists of meaningful relationships with God, family, and friends.

I've shared that sound bite from Jim so many times on TV as we've covered events he attends. I've watched other journalists do the same when they interview him, and the response is consistent: Jim's words speak to all of us.

I have a feeling his birthday celebration is not going to be small. He knows so many people and loves to connect them to one another, so I'm not surprised when he tells me about the plan for his birthday.

"Dianne, I'd like for you and Pete to come to my hundredth-birthday celebration. There will be many people there I'd like you to meet. Plus some of them already know I have been meeting with a journalist, and they'll want to know your story. Would you mind sharing a bit of it during the party? It'll be in the Great Hall at Glen Eyrie Castle, a few weeks before my actual birthday."

I chuckle, thinking about how this man is truly larger than life. Of course it is at the castle. Magical. "We will be there," I tell him.

Jim has so many friends, and he is easily the busiest person I know—of anyone, any age at all. On any given day you can expect his schedule to be filled with at least two or three visits with friends or family members, a school talk about Pearl Harbor, or some other military appearance. One of his favorite invites is to meet with college-student ministry groups. He'll stay as late as 1:00 a.m. if they want to ask questions and swap stories. His schedule from sunrise to sunset looks more like that of a business executive than of a man who is a century old.

Jim simply doesn't tire. I've never seen him ask for a break or need a nap. I've received emails from him late at night, and he'll stay up late to write a note to a friend of mine who needs encouragement. He answers every message he ever receives, not out of obligation but out of genuine interest in each person. I hope I have as many friends as he has when I am one hundred—if I live to see one hundred! What joy to fill your days with people who so delight in you. Jim loves people as individuals, so I imagine his guest list will be legendary.

But that request for me to share some of my story at that party? That's tricky. Rarely do journalists talk openly about their faith. I can't overstate this—we don't talk about it *at all*. So it's a very big deal when my boss, Liz, gives me the go-ahead to speak at a public event for a man of faith. I'm excited to share how Jim changed my life after just a few short months, and this is the greatest gift I can give him: to publicly share what he has taught me, to show that one is never too old to bring people to Jesus.

Brett Clark is Jim's right-hand man, maintaining his schedule and accompanying him to endless engagements. There is no way to keep track of all the events without some help. Brett jokes that Jim's schedule takes the two of them working together to get Jim to so many places and that the heading on the schedule is *Where in the World Is Jim Downing Today?* Brett, along with Jim's caretaker, Carol, faithfully and happily make sure Jim is right on time for every appointment.

As Pete and I arrive for Jim's birthday celebration, the lights of Glen Eyrie sparkle in the setting sun. Glen Eyrie is one of the most magical places I have ever seen. The drive up to the castle is a long, winding, tree-lined road that leads to large rock formations and green, lush lawns and gardens. This is what I imagine the road to heaven looks like. It feels like another world, a welcome retreat from the heartache and crime I report on beyond the front gates.

We walk into the castle front doors, where a giant fireplace welcomes us into the entryway. As we walk up a grand staircase and through several hallways into the

Great Hall, I am energized by connecting with people, and I know an opportunity is waiting in that room tonight. Who knows whether I'll have another chance meeting tonight that will be like the one that brought me to Jim?

The Great Hall doors open to a room fit for a wedding. Large round tables are spread throughout the space, and the room is already packed with people. Jim's birthday is a formal affair—men in suits, women in dresses.

I feel people staring as Pete and I move through the room. I had chosen to wear one of the most conservative cocktail dresses I own, and even still, I feel exposed. The truth is, I don't feel worthy to be here. I'm way too much of a heathen to be in this room of good Christians.

A podium stands in front of a stately stone fireplace. The brown, wood-paneled walls are covered with hunting trophies. It looks like a room in a fancy ski lodge, albeit one with large chandeliers hanging from the ceiling. I've seen pictures of famous evangelists like Billy Graham in that room, with people packed in on the floor and the balcony above.

Jim helped bring this hall—this castle—to life and was assigned by Navigator staff to continue to oversee the Glen after he retired from the navy. The Glen is the ministry training ground for The Navigators, the place they prepare before going out to minister all over the world. It was built in 1871 by the founder of Colorado Springs, General William Palmer. The Navigators bought the seven-hundred-plus-acre estate in 1953 from a Texas oil tycoon named George W. Strake. There is deep history in this room. Tonight it'll be filled with more stories from the past.

I wonder where we will be seated. I assume it is in the back, and I hope the only time people will see me is when I am called to speak about Jim. Just walking in was intimidating enough. This is Jim's night. I want to take a seat with Pete at a back table in the corner and watch as everyone celebrates my mentor.

I spot Jim immediately as we walk in the room, and I smile at his wardrobe choice for his evening of honor: He's wearing a tuxedo and his slippers. If ever a person should be allowed to wear the comfiest footwear he owns, shouldn't it be at his one hundredth birthday? I think how nice it will be to wear slippers with my birthday dress and rhinestone earrings when I'm one hundred.

I can see from a distance that Jim is struggling to hear what people are saying. I watch him ask them to repeat their words as the room fills with more and more people. I suspect he cannot distinguish one voice from another, but the people who haven't seen him in years have no way of knowing about this need. In his classic way, Jim keeps people talking about themselves, smiling and nodding as if he were hearing every word.

I approach him and lean in to say hello and happy birthday—loudly. "Hi, Jim. Happy birthday!"

He smiles at me and says, "I'm so glad you are here."

I hug him, and he shakes Pete's hand. Pete is such a good sport about these events, but I fear he's in for a really long night ahead. What will he say tonight to those who ask him about his relationship with Jesus? I have learned by now how to handle those conversations— I've been studying the Bible every week for an entire eight months—but I worry for him. Pete is still as uninterested in "religy" talk as he was at the introductory lunch we had with Jim earlier that year.

Jim says, "Dianne, you are sitting next to me. Pete, you'll be on her other side, next to the admiral."

Wait. What? I'm not prepared for this. Why didn't anyone tell me ahead of time?

I feel the inquisitive stares—are people wondering why this thirty-five-year-old stranger is sitting next to the guest of honor? My palms sweat and my heart starts to pound. I *do not deserve* to sit next to the birthday man, and WHAT ON EARTH ARE PETE AND I GOING TO SAY TO A NAVY ADMIRAL? Pete's eyes are wide, and I'm searching for any naval information I have in my head.

Jim introduces us to retired Rear Admiral Hank Bond and his wife. "Hello, Admiral Bond," I say. "I'm so glad to meet you, sir."

"Me, too, Dianne. Please call me Hank."

"I can't," I reply, shaking my head. "No, sir. You worked hard to earn that rank, Admiral Bond."

I feel strongly about this in the presence of every military officer I meet. I simply can't address them by their first names—ever.

Pete and I hit it off instantly with the Bonds. They both have friendly faces, and I decide to take Jim's approach to conversation—I'll ask good questions and get them talking about themselves. I've realized over my years as a journalist that I have a gift of being able to get even the shyest person to talk. And I can tell the admiral and his wife are not shy.

As the party gets underway, dinner is served, and someone stands at the podium in front of the fireplace to share stories about Jim. The stories are meaningful and touching, sprinkled with funny moments.

As the second speaker takes the podium, I notice that Jim isn't responding as the rest of us are to the stories. Jim's hearing aids are no match for the acoustics in the Great Hall. He leans toward me and whispers, "I can't hear anything they are saying."

"I wondered about that," I tell him. "I'm sorry, Jim."

I hope he hears my voice when it's my turn to take the podium. If not, he'll still get to see the thank-you note I printed and placed in a folding picture frame alongside a photo of us from the day we met. It also mentions some of the lessons he taught me.

At the right time, I walk to the front with my speech in my hands. I could never ad-lib in a group like this, especially as such a novice Christian. I don't want to leave any room for mistakes.

As I start to speak to the crowd, I take a deep breath. I confess to the room of people, "Oh, my heart is pounding. I think it is easier for me to talk to a television camera than to all of you."

They laugh as I break the ice, and I can almost feel the room exhale.

I say to my friend, in front of all of his friends,

Happy birthday, Grandpa Jim (that's what I affectionately call him). Jim, it is such an honor to be in a room full of people who mean so much to you. Can't you just see the love and feel the kindness in this room tonight?

Meeting Jim is like taking a walk back in history, but the reality is, Jim is so present in each moment. Jim doesn't often talk about the past unless we ask him to—and trust me, I do.

Jim's focus is on now—on Jesus and how he can serve others.

When I asked Jim what he thinks his purpose in life is, he told me that every day he wakes up and figures out how he can spend as much of his day as possible serving others. How selfless. Can you imagine how different the world would be if we all started each day as he does?

Each Tuesday morning, I spend time with Jim, studying the Bible. I was raised Catholic, and for some reason I didn't spend much time opening the Bible. I wish I had, because the peace and the knowledge I have gained from studying only just a few chapters has changed my life forever.

I can't imagine how much better I'll feel once I've read the whole thing, as Jim has. But I'm pretty sure he's read it about a million times.

I now eagerly await my weekly sessions to prepare to learn from Jim. But if you ask Jim, I know he would say I'm not learning from him, but that we're both learning from God.

Everything we have comes from God, and that is one thing I learned long ago. In fact, my husband's wedding band is engraved with the

words "From Him, through me, to you." I hope
Pete has seen a change in me. He encourages
and honors the time I study on my own and
with Jim each week. I hope he sees a more
peaceful and loving wife.

I start to get choked up at the podium. The room
is silent. It is not surprising that I would cry now . . .
I have cried every Tuesday with Jim since we started. I
take a moment to gather myself, and then I say, with a
teary laugh, "I'm pitiful when I talk about Jim."
I begin to read the thank-you letter I printed for Jim.

Dear Grandpa Jim,

*Thank you for introducing me to God. I always
believed in him; I just didn't know him until I
met you. On March 26, 2013, I became a true
believer, declaring my intent to be a Christian
alongside you.*

*Thank you for teaching me to say "I" less
and to focus on others more.*

*Thank you for helping me to understand that
there is nothing to fear, that even in our darkest*

moments, God is with us. You told me that as the bombs exploded at Pearl Harbor, you never once were in fear, understanding that in the most perilous of life's moments, God is right next to us.

Thank you for showing me how important it is to be a good example to others at work, which is really tough in a newsroom. I am sure I fail miserably during the stress of covering the news, but I am working hard at showing my best self to my coworkers.

Thank you for telling me about Mrs. Downing's greatest virtue: her patience. You told me she never lost her patience with you in all of your wonderful years of marriage. What a model to others for how to treat your spouse with true kindness.

Thank you for teaching me the importance of memorizing Bible verses. One of my favorites is Philippians 4:6-7: "Do not be anxious about anything, but in everything by prayer and *supplication with thanksgiving let your requests be made known to God. And the peace of God, which surpasses all understanding, will guide your hearts and your minds in Christ Jesus."*

He smiles and claps, and I'm relieved I can now sit down. This room is filled with admiration for the man sitting next to me, but he doesn't care about the accolades. All he wants people to hear is that the man they are celebrating tonight wouldn't be this full of joy, this full of life, if it weren't for Jesus.

▲ Jim Downing and Dianne Derby, Jim's 100th birthday celebration at Navigators Headquarters, 2013. Photo by Paul Hensley. Used with permission.

▲ Bible study at Garden of the Gods Club, 2015. Jim Downing and Dianne Derby. Photo courtesy of Dianne Derby. Used with permission.

Dianne's Bible. ▶
Photo by Brett Clark. Used with permission.

▲ Veterans Day Parade, Colorado Springs, 2014. From l. to r., Brett Clark, Jim Downing, Dianne Derby. Photo courtesy of Dianne Derby. Used with permission.

▲ Dianne Derby speaks at Jim Downing's 100th birthday party at Glen Eyrie, 2013. Photo by Katie Moum. Used with permission.

▲ Jim Downing baptizes Dianne Derby at the DeRose family home, 2014.
Photo by Katie DiFelice. Used with permission.

▲ Jim Downing baptizes Dianne Derby, 2014.
Photo by Katie DiFelice. Used with permission.

Navy Ball, 2014. From l. to r.,
Brett Clark, Jamie Clark,
Stephany Dyess, Jim Downing,
Dianne Derby, Susan Fletcher.
Photo by Joe Suchman.
Used with permission. ▶

▲ Navy Ball, 2014. From l. to r.,
Jim Downing, Dianne Derby, Susan
Fletcher, Stephany Dyess, Sallie Clark,
Jamie Clark. Photo by Joe Suchman.
Used with permission.

Jim Downing and Dianne Derby, Navy Ball,
2015. Photo by Joe Suchman.
Used with permission. ▶

◀ Dianne and Chip's wedding at Glen Eyrie, 2015. Photo by Teresa Lee. Used with permission.

Election night at KKTV 11 News, 2012. Don Ward, Dianne Derby. Photo courtesy of Dianne Derby. Used with permission. ▶

◀ Colorado Springs Police Department graduation, 2015. From l. to r., Dianne Derby, Chip, Alyssa Chin. Photo courtesy of Dianne Derby. Used with permission.

◀ Birthday party at Lauren Ferrara's home, 2017. From l. to r., Dianne Derby, Claire, Elle Ferrara, Lauren Ferrara. Photo courtesy of Dianne Derby. Used with permission.

Claire's baptism at Glen Eyrie, 2017. From l. to r., Dianne Derby, Claire, Jim Downing, Chip. Photo by Teresa Lee. Used with permission. ▶

◀ Claire's baptism. From l. to r., Steve Rowell, Melissa Rowell, Melissa Piatkowski, Pam Surratt, Chuck Surratt, Claire, Dianne Derby, Chip, Eileen Derby, Bruce Derby. Photo by Teresa Lee. Used with permission.

▲ Jim Downing and Dianne Derby at Jim's bridge-dedication ceremony, 2017. Photo by Cindy Kuhn. Used with permission.

▲ Megyn Kelly interview with Jim Downing, 2017. From l. to r., Dianne Derby, Jim Downing, Megyn Kelly. Photo courtesy of Dianne Derby. Used with permission.

▲ USO Freedom Dinner, 2016. From l. to r., Retired General Lance Lord, Jim Downing, Dianne Derby, Phil Martinez. Photo by Eric Enger. Used with permission.

▲ Dianne Derby interviews Jim Downing in his home, 2016. Photo by Brett Clark. Used with permission.

▲ Jim Downing and Dianne Derby after his interview at home, 2016.
Photo by Mike Petkash. Used with permission.

CHAPTER 7

RESTORE MY SOUL

Devastating Choices and Healing Generosity

THIS IS A VULNERABLE CHAPTER for me to write. I have walked through a darkness that I didn't talk about for a long time, a place where I rejected God, family, and everything I knew to be sensible, true, and right. With my own choices, I created my own form of hell on earth.

I tell you this not because I'm proud of this chapter of my life, and not because I like to talk about it, even after all these years. I'm telling you because I said I would tell you the truth, and that includes the rawest parts of my heart. It is necessary to speak about even this truth, the most painful truth in my story—because meeting with

Jim didn't automatically make me a great person. I didn't change overnight when I started following Jesus.

So here it is: I cheated on my husband, Pete.

For many years I couldn't say that out loud. I now know that an affair is the fastest ticket to hell in a marriage. It is the most evil, selfish, cowardly, disloyal, painful thing I could ever do to someone, and I did it to the man I vowed to love forever. The reality is, an affair doesn't affect just one person. It harms many. So many people get hurt in the shrapnel from that explosion that you can consider yourself blessed if you have any relationships left at the end of it. The only people I had left were my brother, Brian, and his wife, Ashley. It was by the grace of God I had anyone left who knew my truth. They'll never know the depths of my gratitude for guiding me through the agonizing hell I chose.

I share people's mistakes all over the evening newscasts for a living. I headline their choices of evil over good, chaos over peace. While it's never pretty, it pulls viewers in. People love to hate the local preacher's fall from grace, the doctor who got addicted to prescription meds, or the teacher who had sex with an underage student. When we see the poor choices other people make, our own messes seem normal.

Before my divorce, people rarely told me the ugly parts of their soul, the stuff deep down they thought no one would accept. But let me tell you this . . . go through a divorce, and everyone opens up. They find me more relatable, more likable, and, frankly, just as messed up as them. I'm the journalist under the bright lights who can perform well under pressure professionally, but underneath the shiny finish, I am deeply broken like them.

When your face and your voice enter people's homes every evening, they begin to pay attention to the things you're not saying. When a wedding ring is no longer on the left hand of a journalist every night at ten o'clock, people ask questions fast.

The night I take off my ring, the news station is inundated with emails.

"Where is Dianne's wedding ring?"

"Is Dianne's marriage in trouble?"

"Is Dianne Derby single? We thought she was married."

"Is Dianne getting a divorce?"

I ignore them. It's not their business. But they notice. My viewers know even before Jim knows.

The truth is, I don't want anyone to know—but especially not Jim. He's the last person I tell that my marriage is ending. I think, *He's going to discover I'm a lost cause in discipleship, that I can't be fixed, that he's wasting his time. I'm sure he's going to cancel our Tuesdays and be done with me forever.*

And I can't bear the thoughts. He'd introduced me to Jesus. Losing Jim would feel like losing my faith.

But the only thing worse than not telling Jim is the thought that someone else might tell him. I don't want him to know, but I don't want him to *not* know. If everyone else knows, I have to tell my mentor, whether I want to or not.

"Jim, I have to tell you something." My stomach is in my throat. All I have the courage to say is that I am getting a divorce. I wait for him to dismiss me from his life, as I hang on to my darker secret.

His immediate reaction: "Okay, so how do we move forward from here?"

He doesn't judge me. He doesn't dismiss me. He doesn't even question me. He stays by my side, and he mentors me even through this hell I created. His words are just what I need to find a space to cope.

I never tell Jim about the affair, even though I long to feel the grace in his voice, to be reminded that God forgives even my worst sin.

But I can't say it out loud.

———

When my alarm goes off on Christmas morning, the sky is gray, and the weather holds the temperature of snow without the magic of it. I don't spring from the bed, didn't have a night full of visions of sugarplums, and stockings certainly weren't hung by the chimney with care. I'm tired, sad, and divorced. It's my first Christmas alone.

If marriage is a tapestry of stories, memories, and conversations, then divorce is the ragged, frayed fabric of a life torn apart. It's a long list of divided assets and blame. A heart never breaks down the middle, and *amicable* isn't synonymous with *easy*. The "most wonderful time of the year" feels more like a thick fog. I just need to get through it.

When Jim invites me to join him for his Christmas Day tradition, the one he started after his wife passed away, I jump at the chance to welcome his joy into my day. You might imagine his grandchildren sitting at his feet as he reads the Christmas story, squeals of laughter, and songs and turkey and pies, but those aren't the traditions he has in mind.

Instead, he asks me to meet him at the Salvation Army homeless shelter.

There's a long line of adults and children waiting at the entrance of the shelter when I arrive. The director of the shelter holds the door open for me to come inside, and his greeting is the first smile I see on Christmas Day. "Hello, Dianne. We've been expecting you. Mr. Downing is right this way," he says.

I follow him down a hall and into a small room, where Jim sits waiting inside the door. I'm not late, but Jim is always early. He's always ready for the next adventure. Today he's seated next to a long table covered with hundreds of books, and he looks happier than any Santa Claus I've ever seen.

He opens his arms to greet me. "Merry Christmas, Dianne!"

"Merry Christmas, Grandpa Jim. May I join you?" I take the seat beside him, pick up a blue and white book from atop the stack, and flip it open to see the title *The Life of Jesus* from the Holy Bible, King James 1611, by John, His Beloved Apostle. Jim had purchased hundreds of copies of the Gospel of John, and he plans to give each one away.

Next to the books sits a tall stack of crisp five-dollar bills. There must be hundreds of dollars in cash sitting there. Jim says, "I don't know how many people we'll see today, but I wanted to be prepared. Five dollars is enough to do some good without any harm."

He knows it can't buy much, even if it goes to the wrong place.

I smile and laugh. "I think you'll have enough, Jim. This is so generous."

"It's my favorite way to spend Christmas morning," he says. He's been coming here for years and has invited me many times—but I've always been too "busy" (or perhaps too selfish) to join him.

Some local photojournalists wander in behind me. Some recognize me, others don't; I'm not wearing makeup and am dressed casually in jeans and a coat. I clearly am not there to cover the story, but I want to make sure I don't become part of the story either. I know their newsrooms won't want to see me in the background of the video, but this could get tricky since I'll be sitting right next to the guy they came to feature. I approach a few of the journalists I don't know, asking them to keep me out of the story completely. They understand. Actually, they don't really care.

They've drawn the short end of the stick—Christmas Day is one of the worst shifts of the year. Jim's appearance at the shelter is one of the many assignments they'll cover alone today, and they just need to get a quick sound bite and some video of Jim before they're on their way to the next story. In the early part of my career, I worked every holiday for years. It's miserable. News doesn't stop for holidays, and the joy of the day dissipates quickly when you have to work.

The reporters approach Jim to capture some video, and he asks them to keep his name out of the story. I smile when I hear him say this. Jim is a local celebrity, so certainly this community will know who he is when he pops up on their TV screens. They don't need his name to know his face. But the truth is, he doesn't want people to remember him. He wants them to remember the gesture, and he hopes the story might encourage others to start a generous tradition with their own families next year.

The manager of the shelter returns to the room. "Whenever you are ready, I can start sending people in."

"I'm ready when you are!" Jim says.

A line of people trail into the room. True to his nature, Jim greets each individual, learns their name, and spends a few minutes with them. Most of them smile as they meet the old man sitting in front of them, a stranger who has so much more to give than what he's placing in their hands.

Some don't say a word; others whisper a simple "Thank you." Some ask to pray with Jim. He takes their hands in his, and I watch them melt into the comfort of his warmth. He doesn't push them to talk about faith, about Jesus, or about the meaning of Christmas. He simply and completely loves them, with no strings attached. He hands them the Gospel and tucks a five-dollar bill inside each book.

Some people approach with their families, little children with chapped faces and worried eyes. I'm heartbroken at the sight of this—entire families with no place to go. How did this happen to them? Why do these little children have to endure this poverty? I find myself praying, asking Jesus to heal the suffering of these tiny children, so innocent, so small. I want them to have stockings and magic on Christmas morning. My tears well as I see their gratitude for Jim. He tucks extra money into the hands of the parents. He's unwilling to let them go empty-handed.

The line stretches on for two hours, and Jim meets each person as though they were the first one in line. It's as if the man doesn't know how to overlook someone. He truly sees every person.

When the last person leaves the room, I am speechless from seeing one of the most beautiful gestures of kindness to so many.

Jim says, "I still have some more five-dollar bills. I'm going to give them out as I see people on my drive home."

Of course you are, I think. If the people can't come to him, he'll go to them.

I drive away with my spirit soaring. In this, my Christmas of darkness, he has shown me how to lift my eyes above my own circumstances. How to restore my soul with generosity.

In this dark night of my soul, my mentor has given me one of the best Christmas mornings I have ever known.

CHAPTER 8

TURNING THE PAGE

Proof that Jesus Gives Second Chances

A<small>FTER A SEASON OF SINGLENESS</small>, of staring at my mistakes and knowing my truths, of finding my way in the world and learning the sound of my own voice again, I meet someone.

He's one of maybe two men brave enough to come into a weight lifting class filled with women. Chip and I often get stuck in the back of the studio, reracking our weights at the end of class. I say hello one day, commenting on his baseball hat; it says FIRE across the front. I learn that he is a firefighter, and he asks what I do for a living.

It's unspeakably attractive to me that he doesn't recognize me from the evening news. It's a gift to start from scratch with a person, learning about them as they learn about me. A breath of fresh air.

A few hours later, Chip and I have lunch together, and from that moment on, we're inseparable. We are straightforward from the start. We don't play any emotional games, and we don't toy with each other's hearts. They say that's how it is when you fall in love the second time around . . . you know now how hard it can get, how real it must become. Chip and I are honest, we're true, and we fall in love fast.

Soon after we start dating, he gets an invitation, an offer to join the Police Academy. I am not a fan of new risks, but I know this is his dream.

Only a few weeks into his job, my fears are realized. It's the afternoon of Halloween 2015, and Jim and I have just finished our lunch at the Garden of the Gods Club. His wheelchair has barely moved out of the great dining room when I look down at my phone and see that I've missed several calls from Chip's cell phone. Chip NEVER calls me from work.

Chills go up my spine. I start shaking as I call him, even while I'm still in the dining room. He answers the call and says, "Honey, I've been in a shooting."

"What?" I scream into the phone.

My world goes eerily silent for about one second, though it feels like thirty. I'm in a vacuum of the most intense shock and silence. Everything around me is blurry and in slow motion.

"Where are you? Are you in the hospital?" I start to run . . . I want to go to my car, to the bathroom . . . anywhere I can hide.

"No, I'm okay," he says. His voice is even.

"I don't believe you! Are you dying?" The sobs start to set in as I quickly run into the small kitchen off the main dining room. It's not private, but it's the nearest place I can find to escape from the eyes of everyone in the dining room. I sit in a corner of the kitchen, and staff start to swarm around me. I'm crying in my shock, but I don't know any other way to react. "Did you kill someone?" I whisper.

"We did."

I gasp. I cover my hand with my mouth.

"Dianne. He was shooting at people downtown."

"At you?"

"He killed some people."

"Cops?"

"Almost, but no. One cop's car is shot up, but he's okay."

I scramble to my feet. "I'm coming to find you."

"No, don't. I can't talk anymore. I'll tell you everything

when I get back. Chief Carey wanted me to tell you I was okay because all the TV stations are here. We didn't want you to find out that way. I'll call you as soon as I can."

"Okay. I love you," I cry into the phone.

"Love you too," he says.

I do not handle emergencies well, unless I'm on TV. But when it is a police shooting or mass shooting—my hands shake. This time someone I love is at the center of it.

I know the call I have to make next.

"Liz! Chip was in a shooting! He's alive, and that's all I know. I'm going home now."

A few minutes later, my phone rings. It's my fellow reporter and dear friend Alyssa Chin.

"I'm coming," she says. "I'll be there soon."

She is good in stress. So good. When people show up in emergencies, you do not forget that. Alyssa says she'll stay with me until Chip comes back. It's a gift of comfort in a chaos I can't comprehend.

A few hours later, Chip pulls up outside the house. I can hear his truck coming down the street. I jump up from the couch and run outside, right to him. He starts crying as his eyes lock in on mine. We are joined in the tightest hug. I'm sobbing. We're both sobbing. This is too much.

We walk inside, and Alyssa instinctively knows to leave as we process the day's events.

That night Chip and I decide we'll get married the next day. We had just gotten engaged the month before, and we were planning to elope anyway. This moves up our timeline. Chip and I are so thankful he is alive, and we want to make our marriage official.

I email Jim and text Carol.

"Jim, we want to get married tomorrow in the rose garden at Glen Eyrie. Can you officiate?" That garden is sacred space to me, holy ground. I grieved the end of my first marriage among those roses. I want to bring healing to the wound in my life by getting married in the same place.

As usual, he responds quickly. "I'll be there! I can't wait."

And so, on a beautiful November day in 2015, in the presence of only Chip's parents and the great mentor of my life, I become Chip's wife.

———

A few weeks later, there's another mass shooting, this time at the Planned Parenthood site in town. I look at Chip, thankful he is beside me and not at risk this time, but we both ache at the thought of another mass shooting in our community.

I change into my TV clothes and immediately head to work. I stay on-air for the rest of the day. In the end, a local police officer, Garrett Swasey, and two civilians are dead. Several others, including officers, are hurt. The community is shell-shocked, reeling from these two shootings just weeks apart. It's incomprehensible.

I report on the Swasey funeral from the seat of the anchor desk at KKTV, then mute my mic. I begin to sob as his widow and children enter New Life Church in Colorado Springs. I don't know how I'm going to speak on TV after this ceremony. Thank goodness Don Ward is there, sharing the newscast with me. He is a rock of a coanchor in these moments, and after years of sitting by my side, he knows I will not be okay.

As I watch, it's too easy to imagine myself walking behind Chip's casket. I feel myself behind that same podium as Mrs. Swasey speaks about the man she loved. It is too real, too close. Too much. And too many officers are dying this same way.

That night I come home from work and sob for three hours. Chip just holds me, and he doesn't say a word. I don't want to have Mrs. Swasey's story. I don't want our future child or children to face this pain. I can't face it.

Chip always says that if his career becomes too

much, I need to tell him. That day has come, only eight months into his career.

Chip decides to turn in his badge the next day. A selfless act of love.

CHAPTER 9

MARRIAGE TALK

Criticism Is a Dangerous Weapon

I'm THIRTY-EIGHT YEARS OLD and constantly craving Dunkin' Donuts. It's not that I didn't like doughnuts before, but the constant craving is new. Because now, a few months into my marriage to Chip, I am pregnant. And this baby wants doughnuts.

Each time Chip and I walk into a doctor's appointment, I have to stare down the numbers on the scale. Every time, I vacillate between wanting to know and not wanting to know. Wanting to know so I can navigate a healthy pregnancy—but also not wanting to know so I can justify more doughnuts. Chip never looks at the scale. He always says, "Who cares, honey? You're beautiful."

I step off the scale and resign myself to my fate. "I'm getting doughnuts and an iced tea after this. I need a snack." It's my reward for going to the doctor . . . and for anything else I want to reward myself for. On the rare occasions I go to the appointment on my own, I head to Dunkin' Donuts on the way home, order six chocolate-glazed doughnut holes, and devour them before I leave the parking lot.

On a Tuesday morning, in Jim's sitting room, I tell Jim about this routine of mine, and I say, "Chip has never uttered a single word about my weight. He always makes me feel pretty."

"That's a good man," Jim says. "Do you know, Dianne, I've never looked at my wife's driver's license."

"Really? Why?" I ask, considering the weight recorded on my own driver's license. (Everyone lies there, right? I mean, *don't they?*)

"I never looked. Not once," he says.

"She must have appreciated that privacy, Jim."

"Actually, I never told her."

"You just chose to do it on your own?"

"Nobody has to make a declaration to respect someone's privacy. It's just something you can choose to do."

He pauses and then says, "Actually, it's something you must choose to do."

He looks over at the framed portrait of his bride, Morena. It's a large black-and-white photo hanging on the wall in a room they shared, a room that is now his alone. Morena and Jim were married for sixty-eight years. She died in the very room where Jim and I meet every Tuesday. When I look at the photos, I can feel her presence. When I look into his eyes, I can see how much he misses her.

I say, "I can't wait to meet her, Jim. When I get to heaven, I'm going to need at least one thousand years with Morena, one-on-one. That's how long it's going to take me to hear about her Bible studies with hundreds of women, how she managed to raise seven children, and how she handled that terrifying day in Hawaii, not knowing whether her husband was alive or dead at Pearl Harbor."

"She was one in a million. You're going to love her . . . and she will love you." He smiles to himself. "Dianne, can you believe there are some women who want to be considered equal to men?"

Well, that took a turn, I think. I'm not sure where he's going with this. Then he gets a playful smirk on his face and says, "Why in the world would a woman want to leave her lofty throne of womanhood only to descend down to the level of a man with a one-track mind?"

I laugh with him. Even in jest, he keeps Morena on a pedestal. Jim's face lights up whenever he talks about Morena, and he's never made a disparaging remark. Every conversation about her is full of wonder for me. I wish I could have known this woman.

"I've noticed that you never say a negative word about your wife," I say.

"That's another decision I made long ago," Jim says. "Never put your spouse in a negative light to other people, especially in public or in front of the children. It undermines respect when you do that."

"Okay, Jim, let's be honest though. How do you get through it all if you can't vent? Marital conflict is the content of the most hilarious memes on the internet! They make me feel normal. Basically, every day I want to go postal on my husband for some perceived crime I believe he's committed against humanity, like leaving his backpack on our kitchen island." Saying it out loud makes it sound as picky as it really is. I try to justify myself. "There has to be an outlet for my frustration. Just one time, Jim?"

He doesn't budge. (Perhaps he hasn't seen the memes I've seen. Truly on point.)

"There's no one to tell but your partner. It is

devastating for the relationship if you publicly criticize your partner," he says.

I ask Jim to give me the secret to a long and successful marriage since he and Morena were married for almost seven decades. Immediately he gets that smirk on his face, the one that says he's holding a punch line.

"First of all, I'd like to give some advice to husbands," he says, "Never question your wife's judgment. Look who she picked for a husband!" He laughs at his joke, and I love that sound.

Then he adds, "I think the most important thing you can do is express your love for one another, daily and creatively. Leave notes for the other person to find during the day. Give gifts. Use your own creative talent to express love to your life partner. Don't criticize your partner in public, and especially not to other people. If you have the boldness to do that, I think there's an invitation to do it privately. Public criticism is devastating to the relationship. The only person to talk it over with is your partner."

Jim keeps coming back to this last piece of advice, like he knows I need to hear it. I think about this for a long time. I've done well with this for most of my marriage to Chip, but I have to admit . . . this mental shift is tough for me. Sitting with Jim in those moments, seeing the light in his eyes as he talks about his wife, I realize that my behavior in my first marriage was not even close to respectful. Not like how Jim would act, and nothing like Jesus would act.

"Dianne, let's talk about what it means to be a real man or a real woman."

I shrink back, instantly intimidated. Even at nearly forty years old, with a child on the way, I barely feel like a real adult. This is an achievement I assume is only possible when one is as old as the man sitting in front of me.

He says, "A real man or a real woman is secure in all of the relationships in their lives."

All the relationships. *All.* I'm stuck on that word.

"Insecurity happens because we feel uncertain, Dianne. Have you ever run low on gas going someplace? You're not sure you have enough gas to get you to your destination, so you worry the whole way there. When, if you would just stop and fill your tank, you wouldn't have to worry anymore. When we are secure, we are certain."

Man, that's good, I think. I smile inwardly. If only he knew how often I feel insecure. I play a secure person on TV. I know how to look like a secure person, because viewers want someone with that kind of calm and confidence—but they don't really know the real me. I can count the people who know the real me on one hand.

"Have you heard of Dr. Maxwell Maltz?" Jim asks. "He was a plastic surgeon who became fascinated with psychology. After repairing people's outward features, he discovered they still felt rejected. He said the inner self still needs surgery. He wrote books on how to change the inner person as well as the outer person."

This, I understand. My brother is a plastic surgeon, and I was a psychology major in college at the University of Florida. I love to talk about my brother's surgeries, the mind, and why people act the way they do.

Jim hands me a piece of paper with a quote from Dr. Maltz:

The *truth* about you is this:
    You are not "inferior."
    You are not "superior."
    You are simply "You."
    "You" as a personality are not in competition with any other personality simply because there is not another person on the face of the earth like you, or in your particular class. You are an individual. You are unique. You are not "like" any other person and can never become "like" any other person. You are not "supposed" to be like any other person and no other person is "supposed" to be like you.

God did not create a standard person and in some way label that person by saying "this is it." He made every human being individual and unique just as He made every snowflake individual and unique.

God created short people and tall people, large people and small people, skinny people and fat people, black, yellow, red and white people. He has never indicated any preference for any one size, shape or color. Abraham Lincoln once said, "God must have loved the common people for he made so many of them." He was wrong. There is no "common man"—no standardized, common pattern. He would have been nearer the truth had he said, "God must have loved uncommon people for he made so many of them."[1]

DR. MAXWELL MALTZ

Uncommon. I've met so many uncommon people in my career: from the most ignorant to the most intelligent, from the most God-fearing to those who don't believe God exists, from the most evil to the most loving, from the lost to the grounded, from the brave to the cowardly—and everything in between.

"So often we want to be like others, but we have to become ourselves," I say, hoping I'm getting it right.

"Yes," he tells me, "there is something about a secure person that is attractive."

Jim's last statement sticks in my mind: "In our relationship with ourselves, the first way to be secure is to be okay with who we are. Everyone is different, so have you considered how busy God must be? There are 4.17 births per second.[2] And every one is different. The possibility of discovering genetic structures was the numeric total of the population of the earth multiplied to the thirtieth power.[3] So when God gives a genetic blueprint, he throws it away, and it's never used again. Be okay with who you are."

CHAPTER 10

A SACRED GRIEF

Joy in Darkness

I'M FOUR MONTHS into my pregnancy, and Chip and I are beside ourselves with the joy of seeing tiny feet on an ultrasound screen. Everything is progressing well, it seems. But a few minutes later, the ultrasound tech randomly asks, "Has the baby had a nuchal translucency test?"

"Nuchal what?" I ask.

She looks concerned. "I'm going to have the doctor come in."

Immediately a feeling of doom comes over me. I know this isn't good.

The doctor tells us our baby girl—we've begun calling her Claire—likely has an abnormal measurement. The nuchal translucency test will measure the fluid on the back of Claire's neck since it appears to be outside the normal range. The doctor wants to send us to a specialist immediately.

I can't hear any more words. I just want my husband to get me to someone who can give us answers.

Chip drives us to the building next door, the office of a specialist who deals with high-risk pregnancies. I hate the place immediately. No one in the room is there because they got good news; every mother is fighting for her child's life. I want to vomit. The heaviness is palpable.

We are called back quickly into an ultrasound room. A small light hangs above the bed. A technician greets us gently, telling us that her name is Joy. (I have a thing for names, so I find this a cruel joke from God.) She conducts the measurements. I stare at my daughter's body on the ultrasound.

The doctor comes in. She is young and straightforward, and she explains that Claire's nuchal translucency measurement is twice what it is supposed to be.

"What does it mean?" I ask. I need words that make sense.

"It means she has a more than 60 percent chance of being born with a chromosomal disability and a high chance of trisomy 13." As I try to listen to statistics and reports, the doctor's words blend into a mess of noise. She tells me, "If your child lives to be born, she will likely die soon after her birth."

My heart feels like it is going to explode, and I want to wake up from this bad dream. These are possibilities I can't face. I am sobbing as I lie on the table. We were so happy a half hour ago. We didn't know that our visit today would shatter our vision of a healthy child.

The doctor tells me about a test she can do to help her get a greater understanding of Claire's prognosis— but it may cause a miscarriage.

"How many times have you done it?" I ask.

"Four times," she replies.

Four? Another number I can't accept. I appreciate her honesty, but I do not trust her ability. Everyone has to start somewhere, but this is my daughter's life. Four times is not enough times.

I decide I need a specialist with more experience. I will find one. I'm a journalist. I know how to find people.

Meanwhile the doctor explains that this is the time some people decide to end the pregnancy. She says, "This is a Catholic hospital, and we don't do that procedure here."

What "procedure"? She's implying the most tragically

heavy decision, without real words attached. My mind is thick with emotion already, and I can't translate these empty words in real time.

Then I look at Joy's face. Her head is bowed and her lips are moving, and I realize that she is silently praying for my family. Chills go up my spine. I've always said I would never have an abortion, but I am also the type who believes you never really know what choice you will make until you are faced with the decision.

And this is mine: I can't comprehend ending the beautiful life I just saw on the ultrasound.

I will find a specialist. I will find a support group. I am resourceful. I don't want this.

This is the worst day of my life. If the doctor's prognosis is correct, I cannot imagine how I will ever again be anything but sad.

We walk out into the parking lot and get into Chip's truck. I immediately call my mom.

"Something's wrong with the baby." I am crying into my phone.

"What?" She's yelling into the phone. "What do you mean? You just had your ultrasound and sent me the pictures. Everything was fine."

"It's not fine, Mom!" I explain through sobs what the doctor told me.

"Oh my," she says. "I am so sorry, baby."

I hear my dad in the background, responding to my mom's panic, desperate for his own answers.

"There's something wrong with the baby!" she yells to him.

She is starting to get louder and louder. I hear my dad saying, "What, what?!"

They are in disbelief.

"I have to go, Mom. I'll call you later."

"Okay, baby—I love you."

I call my boss, Liz, next. I'm crying into the phone.

"I can't come to work today. I had my ultrasound, and something is wrong with the baby. I can't explain, but please know this is serious."

"Okay, Di, whatever you need to do is fine." Liz and I have become close friends over the years, more than colleagues. She says, "I love you."

"Thank you. I love you, Liz."

"Di?"

"Yes?"

"I know this is painful, but there's something so strong in my heart saying this is going to be okay. I know you don't believe this, but you have to. I just know it. I'm praying for you right now."

"I hope so, Liz. I need your faith. Bye."

When we get home, I immediately message my specialist in Aurora, Dr. Christine Conageski. I am going into problem-solving mode in between tearful breakdowns. She has helped me so often with other health issues in the past. She's the type of specialist whom patients wait months to see. I tell her I am inconsolable, and she agrees to see me next week.

Chip and I walk into the bedroom and fall onto our bed, sobbing. Chip is crying as he lies down next to me on his back, staring at the ceiling. We don't speak.

I want support and I want to support him, but we are useless to comfort each other. He is using all his own strength to keep himself together. We fall asleep in total grief. The night is torturous. Waves of pain and tears wake us over and over. *Will this night ever end?* I wonder.

Morning comes. Relief doesn't. I don't shower. I'm still in my pajamas, and I haven't brushed my teeth or eaten. My phone is full of text messages and voicemails, but I can't respond. I hate everything right now.

My friend Lauren calls, asking to come over. She's one of the few I can even consider allowing into this space right now. "You're walking into hell if you come over. This is pure hell, and I won't be able to fake it for you even for a second," I say. "I'm numb."

"I'll be there soon," she says.

She's at the door thirty minutes later with my favorite chai tea in hand, coffee for Chip, and some pastries to share. She's in her gym clothes and is wearing no makeup. I love this about Lauren. She is my competitor at another TV station in town, but I've never felt an ounce of competition with her. We just don't allow that into our space. We are each other's biggest cheerleaders.

She sits on the couch. I fall into her. She hugs me for a long time while I cry. I explain everything: the stats, the procedure. She doesn't say a lot. Chip is in and out of the living room. He can't bear to see me in such pain, and he isn't going to put on a happy face for Lauren either. Lauren is a positive person, but she knows instinctively that we don't want to see sunshine and rainbows. She knows not to give me false hope. This is heavy and real, and she has walked in so willingly.

God has abandoned me, I think. I feel dead inside. Sleep is a small respite from the pain. It's another night of agony.

The next day, I finally shower. Chip and I head to breakfast at our favorite Mexican restaurant, Rudy's Little Hideaway, a hole-in-the-wall restaurant with concrete floors and dark wooden tables and chairs. Rudy is at the helm, and his family members all work with him. They see immediately that I'm not my typical friendly self, and they seat us at a corner table. I stare out at Pikes Peak as if the beautiful mountain might somehow contain answers.

Chip looks at me and asks, "What if we gave her the middle name Joy?"

Joy is one of the middle names we've talked about—and the name of the ultrasound technician who stayed with us during the bad news. I think back to that moment—Joy's silent prayer, the only light in the room shining down on her head. It felt as if she had been surrounded in light. She was joy in our darkest moment.

"I agree," I say, starting to cry again. "We must speak joy into Claire."

Somehow I know: This baby girl will be our joy. In that moment, Chip and I decide to believe that is possible.

"Claire Joy." I listen to the melody of the words. "I love it."

He smiles. It's the first time I have seen him smile in days.

We finish up our meal, and I tell Chip, "I think I need to go see Jim when we get home."

"Whatever helps, honey. I know how much he means to you."

———

I call Jim's caretaker, Carol. "I need to come over. Something is wrong with the baby."

She asks nothing. She just wants to help. "Come over whenever you want. Jim will be ready."

I make the drive to Mountain Shadows, on the northwest side of Colorado Springs, to the home Jim has lived in for decades. I feel like an empty shell as Carol hugs me. She takes me back to his sitting room.

He sees my sadness and says nothing. I slump into one of the sofa chairs and curl into the fetal position. Carol brings in hot tea, and I take a sip. She treats Jim's guests with such kindness.

Jim will know what to do, I think. This Bible-believing, Christ-honoring, truth-telling lover of God will know what I need, will tell me what to do.

But with the greatest wisdom of all, Jim doesn't tell me what to do. He simply invites me to cry . . . for hours. He sits with me in silence, holding the pieces of my sadness, letting me feel the brokenness of my heart, my family, my life. In his silence, he teaches me the greatest wisdom of sharing a sacred grief: to be present.

In the hours of tears, Jim says nothing. Absolutely not a word. His silence is just what I need. I finally pull myself together. As I am about to leave, he asks if he can pray.

"Yes," I beg.

His prayers always console me. I am still mad at God, but I leave less angry. I leave with a measure of the hope

I always have after being with my friend. I feel his presence is healing, but of course he would say, "That was God healing you."

My eyes are swollen and red with tears as I walk out of his house into the late afternoon. I can barely see the road as I make the ten-minute drive home.

"Did he help you?" Chip asks as I walk in the door. He wraps me in a huge hug.

"Yes," I say.

"What did he say we should do?" Chip asks.

"Actually, he didn't say a word."

In television news, silence is only used for effect. It does not happen often, and when it does, viewers think something is wrong—and it usually is.

Silence outside of television news is different. I've learned it is a gift to the aching heart.

I have learned to love silence now. I crave it. I love yoga, prayer, and meditation for the gift of silence they offer. All day at work I hear the constant hum of televisions, scanners, phones, and doors opening and shutting as reporters leave for and return from reporting stories. I often drive home listening to the spa channel or my favorite pastor on the radio—something calming after a loud, hectic day at work. I need peace and quiet, and I am learning that maybe I need it much more than others.

I've always been curious about what is appropriate to do when someone is suffering. I casually ask people about this all the time, actually. I want to be prepared, and I crave the answers about how they overcome the worst things. Jim taught me an important lesson that day: When someone trusts you with their sadness, just listen. That is how you show up for others in grief.

———

I'm early for my appointment with Dr. Conageski. I can't risk being late. There's too much on the line. In the exam room I tell her what I am facing and how I need someone with experience. She whips out her smartphone without hesitation and calls her colleague Dr. Shane Reeves. He immediately agrees to help me. She tells me Dr. Reeves is who she would want if the same thing happened to her.

A few days later I walk into Dr. Reeves's office with Chip. On the way to the exam room, we pass a wall of pictures, at least a hundred of them: Christmas cards and birth announcements.

This is my sign of hope. I say to myself, *Claire's birth announcement will be on that wall.* We go into his exam room, and he tells me the options. He offers a different test: an amniocentesis. He is so confident it will give us the information we need to know about what Claire is facing. His confidence almost feels cocky, which I find both annoying and reassuring. This man knows his stuff.

"How many times have you done it?" I ask.

"Probably a thousand," he says.

"Now that's the first tolerable number I've heard lately," I say.

He talks me through the procedure and explains how I'll need to take the day off from work because there may be some pain afterward.

"Dr. Reeves," I say, "I need you to know . . . I am deeply depressed. Serious darkness. I am not going to kill myself, but I don't care if I live."

"Do you have a suicide plan?" he asks quickly.

Chip looks at me, worried.

"No," I answer immediately, sure that I won't do that. "I just don't care if I get in an accident and die. I am so sad I cannot get out of this hole."

"Depressed moms have babies with low birth weights," he says, reaching for his prescription pad. "We are going to get you on some antidepressants."

"But what about the baby?" I ask.

He writes the prescription, tears the paper off the pad, and hands it to me. "The risks to the baby are less than your depression."

I take the prescription, and I'll take the pill. I'll do anything to come out of this hole. Anything.

A few weeks later, he calls with the best news we could hope for: The test shows that our baby will likely be okay. I feel unspeakable relief mixed with guilt, since certainly not all moms get this news. And so much remains unknown.

CHAPTER 11

NEW LIFE

Knowing and Seeing Jesus

WE'VE MADE IT all the way to full-term in my pregnancy. Chip and I check in at the hospital at eight o'clock at night. I'm scheduled to be induced, and we're excited to know Claire will likely be here the next day. There's a finish line to the waiting. We settle in for the night, and the nurse, Rachelle, says I can ask for the epidural later, once the pain of contractions sets in.

Epidural: Yes, please. Plenty of women in my birthing class want to do this naturally, but I'm not one of them. Once I feel the pain, I ask for the meds. And as the pain increases, I ask for more meds, and each time I thank God for modern medicine. My goal is to have a baby, ideally without feeling every bit of the pain. (The meds do make me a little bit loopy—my mom tells me later that I FaceTimed her several times with nothing new to say.)

Claire arrives after two hours of pushing, and I'm told I'm lucky it doesn't take even longer. When they place my baby girl on my chest, I think she is the tiniest and most beautiful thing I have ever seen. But she's a little too blue for a little too long. They quickly take her away to get her lungs and blood moving faster. Minutes later she is breathing on her own, her color is good, and she's immediately nursing. My little girl has been born, and she is in my arms.

Two hours after I give birth, as the meds start to wear off and I can walk again, I'm in the recovery room with Nurse Naomi. She is calm and attentive to everything I want or need, and she begins to press on my abdomen to monitor my body's postbirth recovery.

Suddenly she says, "That's weird. Your uterus is off-center."

Two seconds later, twenty nurses and doctors fill the room. I start to hemorrhage. Machines beep loudly, people move quickly, and my head begins to swim. Chip watches my blood pressure drop down to 60/30. Chip is an EMT, and he knows what these numbers mean. I hear him shout, "She's crashing!"

A doctor answers, "We're going to emergency surgery. Immediately."

As they wheel my gurney out of the room, I grab Chip's hand. "Take care of our baby, Chip. You must take care of her. She must know Jesus."

I watch the lights on the ceiling of the hallway as the team races me into the operating room. I call out, praying aloud to Jesus, and begging my doctor, "Please don't let me die." The last thing I remember is a choking sensation as the anesthesiologist prepares to knock me out and intubate me.

I wake up in recovery. While I was in my medically induced slumber, the doctor saved my life.

———

Three years after that unforgettable day, my daughter is smart, curious, and full of words and ideas. We are gearing up for Christmas, and while she's exploring the joy of all that's to come this season, I want to make sure I keep Jesus in front of her. This might be the first Christmas she'll remember.

I pull up a picture of the famous painting of Jesus created by child prodigy Akiane Kramarik. It's a beautiful depiction of his face, so loving. I show Claire, knowing she's never seen this painting before. We do not have this picture in our home, and she's only seen illustrations of Jesus in children's books. I ask, "Claire, who is this?" I'm just curious what she'll say.

My daughter immediately answers, "That's Jesus. But I haven't seen him in a long time."

Wait . . . what?

"Claire, when did you see Jesus? Do you remember?" Honestly, I'm trying not to freak out, but I have to know what she knows. "Claire, when did you see Jesus?"

"On my birthday."

"Where? In the hospital?"

She nods, casually, like she is recalling any other memory that's crystal clear to her. I'll never forget what she looks like in this moment, standing in our living room, wearing her little puppy dog jammies and holding her Woody doll in her hands. She says, "When I was born."

"What was he doing?"

"He was checking on me."

He was checking on her.

"Wow. What did he say, Claire?"

"He was just seeing me, when I was 'sweeping' on you."

"When you were sleeping on me? When you were born?"

She nods.

Oh my goodness. I had begged Jesus to be in that room, to keep my daughter safe. And now I know he was there all along. My daughter knows his face.

———

Claire is just a few weeks old when I bring her to a Tuesday with Jim. More than ever, I want his wisdom to wash over my life. He and Morena raised seven children, and I'm confident of this: A person can't do something seven times over without becoming an expert in their field. I want to know everything he knows.

"Jim," I ask, "how did you and Morena raise seven children? Seven! I can't comprehend this. One newborn dominates my entire life. How do parents—especially single parents—handle this?"

He says, "When Morena and I were raising our children, people often asked about their ages, and I'd say, 'Pick a number; we probably have one at that age.'" He watches me rock Claire on my shoulder. He smiles and says, "You seem much calmer."

"So many of my friends say that, too, that this is the calmest they've ever seen me. Honestly, though, I've been off-air and on maternity leave for two months. I should be pretty calm," I joke.

"There used to be a palpable anxiety about you," he

says, "but that seems to be gone. Many people agree life is much more complete as a parent. Do you find that to be true, Dianne?"

As he says this, I realize I hadn't understood words like this before I had a baby, and now it makes sense to me. Everything seems more peaceful, except for the occasional diaper blowout. My husband and I are so content to have this tiny angel in our lives. After living through the pregnancy worries, and then after surviving a postpartum hemorrhage, gratitude has begun to take root. I pat Claire's back, feeling her warm breath on my neck. "I'm thankful I am alive and our baby is well. Any stress I have now pales in comparison with those scary moments."

Jim says, "I once read a poem written by a new mother, and it was called 'When the Little Tyrant Joined Our Family.' How's that going for you? She probably rules the roost. They dictate when they want to sleep, when they want to eat, and they have no respect for your privacy or routine. You better get used to having a tyrant in your house that you didn't have before." His laugh is so gentle, the voice of a grandpa and a dad who has walked this road so many times over.

Claire has fallen asleep on my shoulder, and I tuck her back into her car seat. She looks so peaceful in her monogrammed white hat with a pink bow, but yes: This tiny tyrant definitely owns me . . . and her daddy.

"Tell me, Dianne, what are you learning?" Jim asks.

"Oh, Jim, where do I begin? I'm learning so much about sleep. I'm told she is an easy baby, but I cringe when people ask me how long Claire sleeps each night. I mean, maybe one to four hours? Why do people care so much about the sleep schedule of a baby who doesn't live with them? It's a surface-level question, basically the same as 'How's the weather?'"

He laughs. "And I do know how you feel about small talk."

"Right? Please, please, STOP ASKING MOTHERS HOW LONG THEIR BABIES SLEEP. Be sure: It's NOT ENOUGH. Leave it at that. And this, Jim— why do people visit for so long? There should be a rule for all visitors: Stay for no more than twenty minutes max, unless you are coming to hold or feed the baby so Mom and Dad can actually sleep. Honestly, Jim, each day there's a line of people waiting who want to smell her sweet baby head."

"And they don't know when to stop, do they?" He smiles.

"Jim, some of them stay for two hours. If you are visiting for ninety minutes—yes, I had several of those visitors—I assume you have not had children, or you must be so far removed from having a newborn that you can't remember. Please get these important boundaries for those of us, like me, who are not good at enforcing them when we are tired. I promise I'm saying this all with a kind heart . . . except to the ninety-minute lingerers. Clearly I'm not over them. Real calm, huh?"

He smiles. "It's all part of the process, learning how to love all the people who want in on the love you have for your daughter."

"Jim, that's just it—more than anything, I want Claire to feel loved. I want Claire to know I'm always happy to see her, and I want her to know that I will love her through any challenge we face. My goal as a momma is to immediately smile with my face and my eyes every time she enters a room. I mean, it's easy right now . . . but I want to be that way always, even when she's a teenager who doesn't like me anymore. I was so tough on my parents during those years. I was happy to please them as an excellent student, and on my terms. But when it came to my freedom, oh, let me tell you, Jim, I fought hard for any ounce I could get. In my mind, it was never enough. Plus, they had to be some of the strictest parents in my school, or so I thought back then. I want Claire to know that I light up over her."

Jim says, "Every generation thinks their children are the worst and the most disobedient. I read about an artifact, an Assyrian tablet from five thousand years ago, where it was written, *The earth is degenerating these days, there are signs civilization is coming to an end, bribery and corruption abound, violence is everywhere, children no longer respect and obey their parents.*"[1]

"That hasn't changed much," I reply. My next question is a tender one. "Grandpa Jim, will you baptize Claire?"

"Well, I don't usually do baptisms for children," he says. "It's important for a person to choose a life of faith on their own; but for Claire, I'll make an exception. It's called a dedication."

So when Claire is only a few weeks old, family members travel from all over the country to Colorado Springs to witness this special moment. Jim arranges for Claire's dedication to happen at Glen Eyrie, a most fitting, sacred location for this most sacred moment.

I feel an urgency based on Jim's age and my mother-in-law's failing health; Pam's breast cancer has returned. Time has become more precious, and I know how much she wants to witness this.

Pam is an elder in her church, and she glows in that environment. When most of her family comes to town for Easter and attends the services on Sunday, a few months after Claire is born, she almost vibrates with excitement. She buzzes around the church, proudly introducing each of us to the members. It's the same church in which I will eulogize her when she loses her final battle with breast cancer two years later.

The morning of Claire's baptism holds even greater gravity when our doctor calls and tells us that Claire does not have Turner's syndrome. When I was pregnant, we had worried about so many things, and even after Claire was born, there was one more test to rule out any possible birth defects. The doctor's call that morning confirms it: negative for Turner's. I breathe out the greatest exhale. My daughter is healthy and will be dedicated to the Lord. This day is getting better by the moment.

When we get to Glen Eyrie, I meet my family at the top of the stairs inside the castle. My sister-in-law, Melissa, quickly sweeps Claire into her arms. She is instantly in love. She left her family in Nebraska behind to be here for this last-minute moment. She'll never understand how much it means to me. Chip's aunt Melissa and uncle Steve from New York didn't want to miss it either. They're the family members who say yes to any event I invite them to, and they make it happen at a moment's notice. They appreciate how much time with family means to me. Of course, my parents are there too. They always—always—show up even though they live across the country. It's such a treasure to have that from them. And Chip's parents smile on, the moment bittersweet and immensely precious, as each family moment is while time fades for Pam.

Jim welcomes us all into a room and begins the dedication. I can tell Pam is tired but is putting her best smile forward.

We are all following Jim's lead. I love every second, hanging on every word he says. I feel a beautiful joy as I watch each person pray over our baby. Afterward, we go outside the castle to take family photos with Jim. One of the pictures will eventually hang in the front hallway of my home, a permanent reminder of the life of faith I intend to share with Claire—and of the man who led me to it.

CHAPTER 12

SO LONG, DEAR FRIEND

Discipling until the End

SOME PEOPLE STOP LIVING long before their last breath. They stop using their muscles and their appetites, they stop making their choices and using their voice, and they give up and check out before their lives are finished. But not my friend Jim Downing. His life matches his days. Even in Jim's final year—at "104 and a half," as Jim proudly declares—his schedule is still filled with meetings.

Brett Clark often tells me, "One-oh-four has a big schedule today." We both just laugh at the thought of a 104-year-old man with such a full to-do list. Jim doesn't stop learning, growing, and loving with his heart, soul, and mind, even as his body grows tired toward the end.

In those last days, Jim's caretaker is inundated with requests to see him. People go in and out of his home all day long. Each person wants more, but as the days get closer to the end, fewer people are allowed in.

On one of our last Tuesdays together, he is weary, and I can see it. I ask him whether there is anything I can do for him, anything that would help him at all. In true Jim Downing style, he asks me to reply to his emails. He can neither read nor respond to the dozens of emails he receives each day anymore, though I've never understood how he could in the first place! Jim used to stay up late at night, typing away at his computer just to make sure each person received an encouraging note. Now it's bothering him to think about those messages going unanswered, unattended, just accumulating in his in-box. Even while he faces death, he is others-centered.

So I grab his iPad, and I get to work writing his final letters. I read each message aloud to Jim, and I dictate his reply. I let each person know that Jim has specifically asked me to contact them on his behalf, even as he is in his final days and unable to write. What sacred space, that he trusts and allows me to speak on his behalf for his parting words to so many.

He asks me to email one of my friends, a soul sister of mine who has become a friend of his as well. She battles alcoholism, and Jim prays continually for her to find a way out of her addictions. He is always encouraging, always praying for, always pointing each person back to the one answer he gives: Jesus. His answer is always Jesus.

On the last day of his life on earth, his family invites me to come to his house. My throat tightens with the phone call. I know this is the end, and I don't want it to be.

It is peaceful and serene in his home. Jim lies in the same room where his wife passed. Soft music plays in the background, and the air smells of beautiful incense. Jim is sedated, and he doesn't look anything like he did just weeks before. He's so small and frail in that bed.

I take his hand one last time. I pray for him out loud and tell him I love him, and I give him a kiss goodbye on his forehead. I'm not sure if he hears my words, but Jim already knows how I feel.

His family members come in and out of the room, but no one is crying. They know his time has come. Jim has lived a life so devoted to Jesus, there is no doubt where he is going. One of Jim's grandsons plays a guitar at his bedside, the hymns and songs Jim loves. This gesture of kindness makes my eyes swell with tears. I sit back in a chair, and I just listen, watch, and take it all in. I'm still, in awe of so much beauty, as Jim lies in the space between his earthly presence and eternity with the one he loves more than any other: Jesus. Jim has always told me that Jesus is the best spouse, friend, brother, sister, father, mother that we could ever have. And finally, Jim is about to meet Jesus face-to-face.

I slip out quietly that afternoon, going on to the studio to report the evening news. Just before I go on the air, Jim's daughter-in-law texts me to say Jim is gone. I pause and thank God for my time with my friend. I take a few deep breaths, thinking of the glory he is experiencing now, his arms wrapped around Jesus. It is the day before Valentine's Day, and I like to think Jim was able to give a valentine to his sweetheart, Morena.

The last time I see Jim, he's lying in his casket in the Shrine of Remembrance in Colorado Springs, the same place where his wife lay in rest in a mausoleum. Jim's twin sons greet me at the door. I'm always intimidated by these two impressive men, but they welcome me as family.

Jim's daughter-in-law Debbie greets me with such warmth as well. She's like the comforting best friend you want to see when you're in pain. "Do you want to go see

Dad?" she asks. I nod. She takes my hand and walks me to his side. I touch his lifeless hand and tell him how sad I am to see him in a casket.

———

Jim's funeral is a star-studded memorial service of a life well lived. His family invites me to speak, to give a public farewell to the man who changed my life. This is what I share in front of a crowd of several hundred people packed into the Great Hall at Glen Eyrie:

> I am certain when Jim saw Jesus' face for the first time, Jesus said to him, "Well done, good and faithful servant. Well done."
>
> Jim's life from 22 years old until 104 was filled with serving Christ, even until his final moments, worrying about making time to see those who wanted to say goodbye, to meet their needs instead of his. He wanted to pass on the wisdom of God in any way he could, to have one more opportunity to be a servant of the Lord. Such selflessness.
>
> Jim told me that when he gets to heaven, he wants to thank God in person for sending his Son to die for him. He said he'll also thank God

for answered prayers. Jim and I talked about heaven a lot. I loved to talk about what it must be like. Don't we all want to know? Is it possible to be at peace, have that unending joy? Yes, and it's possible on earth too. That's what drew me to Jim.

Shortly after I met him, he said, "Do you want to meet someone who is totally fulfilled?" Of course I did.

He said, "You're looking at him."

Well, let me have some of that, please. And so began our one-on-one Bible studies almost every Tuesday for the next five years.

During that time, I wrote down so much of what Jim said. The front and back of my Bible, which I did not have before Jim, and the pages inside are filled with notes I quickly wrote down as I tried to soak in his wisdom. I want to share just a few of them with you.

- Love is the voluntary giving up of oneself to another.

- Never criticize your partner in front of anyone, including your children.

- People lie because of a lack of courage.

- Alcohol is the devil's substitute for the Holy Spirit.

- Pride is the worst sin in the Bible. It is preoccupation with oneself.

- Sometimes we put a higher priority on worrying than praying; 92 percent of what we worry about never happens.

And on a tiny piece of paper I've had in there for five years, he had typed out, "God may have created man before woman, but there is always a rough draft before the masterpiece." He loved to laugh and always knew how to make us laugh along with him.

The final verse he sent to me on Sunday was John 14:1: "Let not your hearts be troubled. Believe in God; believe also in me."[1] What a beautiful verse to share at the end of his life.

I waited five years to write this, hoping and praying that somehow this day wouldn't come, that my tiny little daughter would know him the way I do, that I'd get more time . . . that we'd all have more time. But I am deeply grateful for the time I had, and I can't wait until we meet again.

———

Jim Downing showed me who God is—because he showed me no-strings-attached love. The book of 1 John says that over and over: that God is love, and that we show who God is by loving each other. That's why I wasn't scared when Jim asked me to start learning from him on Tuesdays. Love made our conversations real, not "evangelistic."

Jim modeled a life of discipleship that is a rare and beautiful find, and when he scooped me up as his mentee, he changed my life. He had been making disciples for more than seven decades by the time I met him, which is funny because he didn't even really like the word *discipleship*. He said it was overused and a little worn out, and its vague meaning meant something different to each person. Instead of discipleship, he liked the idea of "multiplication" or "spiritual reproduction." In the world of nature, when an animal or a plant is mature, it reproduces itself. Jim saw himself as a parent to young believers, and he parented me into emotional and spiritual maturity. Jim knew that the key to loving a child well is to know them well, and he extended that to me, as his honorary granddaughter.

When you spend every Tuesday morning with

someone for five years, you learn a lot about each other. "It takes more than a howdy and a handshake to know someone," Jim once said to me. "How well we know another person is relative to the number of shared experiences with them and the depth of those times together."

Depth. That feels like the magic word. Jim never once—never once!—wasted time on small talk. Talking about the weather makes me tune out in about five seconds, but someone's thoughts, inspirations, what they crave most in life—this I could talk about for hours and hours. And we did. Every time I showed up to meet with Jim, I was changed before I left the room. That's the power of the presence of someone who was walking with Christ, passing his faith on to someone who wanted to learn.

Jim had such a sense of approachability. I wanted to learn from him because I wanted his joy. I could feel it when I was with him. He was always so interested and invested in others. He would remember things I told him for weeks afterward. Jim showed me how that kind of intentionality made people feel. When he would come to an event with me, he'd be by my side, and I would watch others enjoy him. The closest people in my life got to know him too. And they loved him.

Jim continues to mentor me, even after his death. His

stories and teachings wove their way into my memory when I didn't even know I was listening. They pop up now in my daily life.

- **Worry:** When I lay awake at night, feeling worried about the world and the future it offers to my daughter, Claire, I can remember Jim saying, "Worries are self-manufactured, and most of what we worry about never happens. Our worries are in our imagination, not in the realm of reality. This is why people need to memorize the Serenity Prayer." (Twice Jim wrote down the Serenity Prayer for me. Both are taped to the inside cover of my Bible.) Prayer was his go-to answer for worry.

  Jim also told me he navigated worry by imagining the worst-case scenario. (The worst-case scenario is literally my go-to thought pattern every second of my life. I've pictured it, I've reported on it, and I probably know someone it's happened to.) When Jim was the captain of a navy ship during the Korean War, he once had a mission to dock the ship in a place where a typhoon had broken most of the pier away. There were rocks on each side and no tugboat. He was sure he was going to run this ship into the rocks and aground, perhaps killing someone. If any of that happened, he'd get a court-martial and never receive a position of responsibility again. That was the worst-case scenario. But that's when he realized that no matter what happened, he'd still be okay. He would not be without the love of God or his family or his relationships with friends. As Jim said, "When I consider this, I can live with the worst-case scenario."

- **Relationships:** When Chip and I cannot see eye to eye, I recall what Jim would say: "Love is the voluntary giving up of oneself for another. It is unconditional acceptance and desire of good for another person." Chip demonstrates this far better than I do. He's so accepting and selfless in our marriage. He makes me and Claire feel like we are the two most important girls in his life every single day. He makes me want to do everything so much better.

  Jim taught me that "the permanent foundation of a relationship is mutual respect." When respect is gone, the relationship is over. I've seen this in romantic relationships and work relationships; once I lose respect, the relationships often end . . . or slowly fade. That kind of loss can require so much patience to rebuild, and sometimes it can't be recovered at all. When respect is on the line, the risk is too high.

- **No Substitute:** Jim never had a drink of alcohol, as far as I know. It was a simple decision for him. He didn't need it. He was so alert, so present with everyone he met. He wanted to have the depth of friendship that comes without the influence of alcohol, the true transparency that can be clouded by intoxication. Jim was on to something. He taught me when you have Jesus, you don't need any lesser things to help you cope. Jim believed *God* is the answer. *He* is the ultimate comfort, the ultimate peace. There is no substitute for the Holy Spirit.

- **The Greatest Bridge:** I think of Jim every time I drive on the I-25 bridge over Cimarron Street, right near downtown Colorado Springs. This is the largest bridge in Colorado Springs, and it is named after Jim: Big green signs on both sides of the interstate announce the "Lieutenant James 'Jim' Downing Bridge."

  The bridge-dedication ceremony was in a park just east of the bridge on a cool fall morning in 2017. Jim was in his full navy uniform, ready to accept the dedication on behalf of all the heroes before and after him. After he thanked the people who organized the dedication and honored the veterans of the past, he left us all with one final, breathtaking quote:

"The greatest bridge is the bridge between heaven and earth."

Jim was honored by the bridge dedication but, as always, found a way to show others God was first in his life. Pointing to the "greatest bridge" was one of his final public acts of faith.

At more than one hundred years old, my mentor told me, "I've still got plenty of life left." And right up to the very end, Jim was still teaching, still growing, still chasing down life. One of my biggest challenges every day is to live the example Jim has set for me—and I know Jim would clarify right now: "Dianne, you mean the example Jesus has set for us." He had a unique ability to demonstrate grace and truth at the same time. I try to live that in my life, to create an environment that is loving and supportive, a space that Jim would be proud of—and that Jesus would be proud of.

Jim helped me finally understand compassion, kindness, courage, loyalty—everything you can think of that Jesus is. He went after the needs in my hungry heart, and all the while he was teaching me the stepping-stones of a life of faith: reading, studying, memorizing, meditating on, and applying the Word of God. He showed me that the greatest disciples—followers of Jesus—are those who love Jesus more than family, more than career, more than material things. They identify with the things of Christ, and they are his representatives in the world. It's a high calling that I'll forever aim to live up to, and Jim Downing set the example.

As Jim has entrusted wisdom to me, I now also have the privilege and the responsibility to pass it on to others. I have that opportunity every day as I encounter all kinds of people. I suppose I don't preach to the world; I just live by that example. There's no greater way to show God's love than to show what he's done and changed in you—and by living that example to others.

I don't have to be Jim Downing. I don't have to do it his way. (As I write this book, I've only memorized two more verses.) But to just talk openly with the people in my life, the people I love, about what I am learning . . . to be one or two steps ahead of the person I'm trying to help . . . that's how I can pass life and wisdom and the love of Jesus on to someone else—just the way Jim did for me.

TOTALLY FULFILLED

"When I get to heaven, one of the first people I want to see is Virgil Hook. He's the one who helped bring me to Jesus."

It's hard to imagine a time when Jim didn't know Jesus, to imagine that someone had to introduce him to the Savior he shared with me. I guess we all start somewhere. He was an acorn before he was an oak tree.

Jim told me, "We were on work duty, and I remember Virgil and I were handling frozen beef. It was a hard job, an unbecoming task, and I was angry about it. But Dianne, do you know what I noticed? Virgil's face was shining. He was humming a tune and having the time of his life."

"Holding frozen beef?"

"Yes," he said. "Isn't that amazing? He was just happy as could be as we were stuck with this mundane task. I knew he had what I wanted: an inner resource to cope with all the outer circumstances. I had to know more."

"That's like when I met you, Jim," I said.

When Jim told me he was totally fulfilled, he wasn't exaggerating. I've never known a person more content with his life. "I have a formula for fulfillment," he told me. "I call them the Four Ds. The first one is *Discover your gift*. Discovering your gift and who you are—this one is often the hardest."

I pondered this, replying, "When I was in college, it was so hard to know what I wanted to do for the rest of my life. I knew I wanted to be a journalist, but I didn't have the guts to do it. I lived through my sorority sister, Erin Andrews, who was chasing the dream and eventually made it big. Why is it so hard to discover your gift?"

"It sounds like you knew what you wanted to do, but you needed courage. Even there, though, you're an exception. At least you've known what you wanted to do from the beginning. Most people don't know. Young boys often want to be truck drivers at first. Then they want to be pilots, aviators. But many of them are not equipped to do that. I feel the best way to discover your gifts is to consult with someone who knows you and loves you, someone whose life you have influenced. They have the courage to be objective, and they will tell you where you come across strong and weak. The people who know you and love you will give you a clue to what your gifts are."

I was curious. Jim had lived such a rich life and seemed to have such clarity about what he was meant to do. "How did you discover your gifts?" I asked him.

"I invited my three closest friends to evaluate me. It's hard for family members to be objective, so I didn't ask them. I asked my friends. I said, 'Please tell me how I come across to you. To make it easy, put it in the format of strengths and weaknesses. How do I come across as strong, and where do I come across as weak?'"

"You must have really trusted them. That's a vulnerable question to ask, to tell you the truth."

"Well, to be honest, they weren't very comfortable with it. They didn't want to do it. So I said, 'Let's do it anonymously. Each of you write it on a card, and then we'll have my secretary type it, so I won't even see your handwriting.' And they did.

"Just before doing this, I spent some time in personal evaluation, looking at my strengths and weaknesses. When these cards came in, I got the shock of my life. What I thought was a primary strength, all three friends classified as a major weakness. And two of the things I thought were weaknesses, they named as outstanding strengths! I was shocked. I am convinced that no person can be objective enough to effectively evaluate themselves. You need to invite someone on whom you've made an impact."

I asked, "Was it clear to you after that?"

Jim replied, "Yes. I retired what I thought were my strengths, and I brought out of retirement the things they said were my strengths."

He continued. "The second D is, *Dedicate your gift to a higher purpose than yourself.* Find a way to invest in the lives of others, and join God in what he is doing in people, in relationships, and in the world. Next, *Develop your gift to the maximum.* Do whatever you must to become an expert in your field, to achieve excellence in your craft. And finally, *Deploy your gift.* Everything that's ever been created has been created for a purpose. When something is fulfilling the purpose for which it is created, it is, at that point in time, perfect. By discovering and deploying our gifts, we are doing what we are made to do."

"That's so good, Jim," I said. "And it can be so hard to find. It took me a long time. I earned two master's degrees before I figured out what my gifts are. As soon as I picked the gift that I knew had been in my heart for so long, everything fell into place."

"A Greek philosopher once said, 'The world steps aside to make room for the person who knows where they are going.'[2] Dianne, a secure person has that image. They know where they are going."

"Oh, Jim. This I get . . . well, at least the 'going' part. I knew exactly where I was going when I decided to become a journalist. Nothing stopped me. I followed every step and every piece of advice to get there. Everything flowed. EVERYTHING. I encountered plenty of challenges along the way, but nothing stopped me."

"That's a strong sense of direction," he said.

"But it wasn't easy. The first challenge started with a journalism professor, before I even got accepted to his graduate program. I asked to meet with him to learn more about the program, and as I sat down in his office, he immediately said, 'You know this business is more than just a pretty face.'"

Jim raised his eyebrows.

"Right? I told him, 'Yes, I understand. I already have one master's degree. I'd like to get one more.'"

"Good answer," Jim said. (Mental gold star.)

"Thank you. He was the grumpiest man I have ever met, but I had to learn from him. He certainly wasn't going to sugarcoat anything on my behalf."

"And did you get into the program?"

"I sure did. A few weeks later, I got my acceptance letter in the mail."

Jim nodded. He shared, "I once read of an eighteenth-century author who said, 'There is something about conviction that makes beauty out of the commonest of clay.'[3] So, real beauty is the beauty of conviction."

Jim's wisdom remained with me long after his death, meeting me in moments I could never have anticipated. And in those moments, I learned something more: The wisdom of a man like Jim is only the beginning of the path to total fulfillment. On that day when I talked with him about my purpose, I thought journalism, the endless yeses, was the center of it. That, I thought, was my way forward to total fulfillment. But Jim was never talking about doing. He was talking about being, about who we are wherever life takes us.

And in the season of my life when his absence felt like a gaping wound, I started to understand that particular lesson.

———

It's 2020, several months into a global pandemic. I'm finishing a newscast when I receive an emergency text from the station's management: All-staff meeting in five minutes.

The newscast had been over for only five seconds. Meet in the studio in five minutes? *We're all getting fired*, I think. There's no other explanation for all of us being called to the newsroom—even the people who are quarantined are told to join us on Zoom. Everything is inexplicably frantic.

As people enter the studio, I study them for clues. The manager's eyes are red and rimmed with tears, and one of my colleagues is openly sobbing. I ask him, "Tony, what's happening? Are we getting fired?"

"I don't know. I don't know." He just keeps repeating, "I don't know, I don't know." I push him to tell me, but he won't do it. Can't do it.

When I see the vice president of the station come around the corner, I know something is very, very wrong. He was the general manager during the Waldo Canyon Fire, and when he showed up *then*, we were in the heat of an emergency. If he's in this meeting, something is horribly wrong.

I look at him and basically shout, "Nick, what's happening? What happened?"

His face looks pained. He says, "This is so sad, and I don't know how to tell you this." And then he begins to cry. "Don Ward died today."

Don Ward. My other half in the newsroom. Gone.

Don had been on a quest for health. He had stopped eating the goodies in the newsroom, and he'd limited himself when I ordered cheesy bread almost every Friday night. He had lost weight and beaten his diabetes diagnosis, and hiking had become his hobby. At the end of every newscast, he would walk out with me to make sure I was safe in my car before he left for the night, and this last time he'd told me where he would be the next few days—off to climb a chain of three mountains. I told him to enjoy his time off.

He died on one of those mountains. My coanchor is gone.

I lie down on the ground and sob for nearly an hour. I weep for his family, his nieces and nephews, whom he loved like they were his own children. *They were the center of his world, and now he is gone.*

I cannot be consoled. Shock and grief crash over me like waves. My heart physically aches. I feel broken that I didn't get to say goodbye.

I call my husband. I call my mom. I can't even

believe my own words each time I hear myself speak: "Don's dead."

And I have to go on the news in just a few hours. I have to tell our community that he is gone. How will I tell them? How will I do justice to this story?

It is a dark day in our city, in the newsroom, and in my heart.

I write a eulogy to deliver at his memorial service, but I'm unable to share it. In the days between his death and the funeral, another crisis happens. I'm standing in the studio, recording a commercial to inform the community about Don's memorial service, when a motorized camera sweeps in from my left side and crashes against my head. The blow throws me to the ground with a concussion. Since we are recording, the whole thing is captured on camera—the collision, my fall, and my weeping on the floor with a head injury.

I'm hospitalized for the concussion, and I tell the doctors that my heart hasn't stopped hurting since Don died. I'm scheduled to see a cardiologist next week, but the emergency doc recommends answers sooner. When the blood work shows symptoms of a heart attack, they do a procedure to enter my heart and assess the damage. I'm awake during the procedure, lying on a table in the cardiac catheterization lab. The faces around me are all business, and I know I have the A-team, who were awakened in the middle of the night to explore the inner workings of my heartbeat.

This is what they tell me later: My heart stopped pumping properly upon the news of Don's death. They call it "a stress cardiomyopathy," appropriately also named "broken heart syndrome."

Liz Haltiwanger reads the eulogy on my behalf. Everyone assumes I'm too grief-stricken to show up at the funeral, but I'm stuck in the hospital bed under the orders of my doctor—awaiting an MRI, not permitted to even watch the service on my phone. My heart *literally* cannot handle the sadness.

Because of the pandemic, the rules in the hospital are fierce. Nobody is allowed to see me, except for one guest per day. Chip is home with our daughter, so my mom books the first flight from Florida to Colorado, as my one guest.

My cardiologist makes direct eye contact with me. He says, "When these health concerns arise, many people consider changing careers. You have got to make some changes, Dianne. You must take care of yourself, and you must slow down."

I hear Jim in my head: *Be still.*

I never slowed down, not for a moment, and now it has come to this. I have no choice now.

I lie in my hospital bed, alone in my room, wishing to talk to Jim. I want to tell him how unfair it all is: The pandemic. Don's death. And now I have to give up the gift I thought I was born to offer the world.

But I know what he would say. When I'd ask him why awful things occur, he'd say, "Dianne, the unexplainable happens to glorify God."

For a long time, that answer made zero sense to me. Pandemics that kill, people who hurt children, hearts that break, cancer that ravages the body, buildings that collapse with people inside, infernos that sweep through cities—how could any of those glorify God?

I could not give simple, pat answers frosted over with the word *glorify*. I needed more. I needed it for the people who were listening to the nightly news, and now, alone in the hospital bed, I need it in my soul.

In my questioning, I turn to God. That's what Jim would tell me to do. (In fact, he's probably glad to be out of range, so I will turn to God after all.)

In a moment of clarity, I sense an answer.

Dianne, let me help you understand. You live in a world broken by sin and illness and destruction. Bad things happen all around you, and those are not what glorify me. Those things break my heart. But when my people love each other in the hurt, when they look to me with trust, when they run toward the emergency instead of away from

*it, when they love each other to their healing—that's when
I am glorified. It's not the pain that brings me glory . . .
it's my people loving me and loving each other, even when
it hurts.*

For the first time, so many things make sense to me.

As our community grieves the loss of Don, they also
weave an imperceptible yet tangible safety net underneath
me and my colleagues. People write letters and notes, send
packages and meals. Behind the scenes at the station, the
studio looks like a floral shop. We do not grieve as those
who have no hope,[4] and we do not grieve alone.

Before now, I thought I needed to keep all the plates
spinning to cover the news, meet the expectations, and
live my best life. I thought total fulfillment lay somewhere on that path, on the conviction of my journalistic
integrity, on that particular calling.

But as it turns out, the next step to total fulfillment
is just as simple as Jim always told me:

Trust God.

Love the people around you.

Be still.

———

If I learned anything from Jim over our two hundred
Tuesdays, it's this: Fulfillment is a multifaceted gem, the

pieces of a life lived well. It's layered and beautiful—and yet at the end of the day, incredibly simple.

"Remember how I told you I'm so content?" he asked me once. "That's because Virgil Hook introduced me to Jesus. My life changed because of him. I think he'll be one of the first people I look for in heaven."

Virgil was Jim's "Jim." Virgil showed him the path toward being totally fulfilled. And Jim did the same for me. I get to walk that path just as Jim did—imperfectly, ever forward, moving toward Jesus the whole time. That's where I'm going to find true fulfillment: in deep relationship with God, family, and friends.

Jim believed that heaven is friendship-based. He said, "Dianne, when I get to heaven, I'm going to ask Jesus for a reunion planet. There are so many conversations, so many moments I want to re-create that I'd like to have my own planet where these moments start up right where they left off. Can you imagine how much fun that would be? Think of all the times you've met someone and had to end the conversation because it was time to go, but you left wanting more. All of that would be fulfilled there."

I imagine this planet. There are tables set up near waterfalls, and there is the smell of fresh flowers everywhere you go. The planet is warm and green and is filled with the beautiful sounds of wildlife and music.

Everyone I love is there, and we are happy and at total peace. This is the reunion planet I crave.

I took Jim's hand. "When I get to heaven, I think I'll find you and Virgil both."

He smiled, and his eyes sparkled once again.

"We'll be waiting."

ACKNOWLEDGMENTS

I WANT TO THANK my parents first. They are my biggest cheerleaders. There is no one who thinks I am more amazing or talented than my father. He is the loudest and proudest father there is, and he will tell everyone he knows. My mother is the parent who always pushes me to stand up for myself and demand the best from everyone around me. I have achieved so much in my career because of their endless help and sacrifices. They are the most wonderful parents I could ever imagine calling mine.

Thank you, Don Pape—champion of words, master networker, and mentor of mine who has made a dream come true.

I thank my agent, Greg Johnson, who welcomed me into his world with open arms and championed my story. Greg, I sat in your office that first day praying, hoping, and dreaming. How blessed I am that you took our book idea so seriously.

I thank the team at NavPress, who invited me to a luncheon to meet a team of superstar authors. I felt my world shift in those moments, and I knew something amazing was about to happen. One of those superstars, Tricia Heyer, became my coauthor. This book is the result of your belief in me.

I thank my editors at NavPress: Caitlyn Carlson and Elizabeth Schroll. You make everything shine. You are two of the smartest women I've ever met, and you have a loving-kindness with your critique and edits. I pray to be as gentle and eloquent as you when editing scripts in my newsroom.

I thank my coauthor, Tricia. You have spent countless hours making my words and my story come alive on the page. You made me feel heard and accepted from the moment I met you. Thank you for listening to me talk about my happiest and darkest hours and helping me to make sense of it all. Your friendship is an unending hug for my soul.

I thank Melissa Rowell. You were my first editor of this book. You scrutinized every word and finished an enormous task in no time. Your life continues to bless mine over and over. I am so thankful to call you part of my family.

I thank my husband, Chip. You have shown me and our daughter that love is selfless, intentional, and full of laughter. You are my proof that God gives second chances. I treasure sharing all my days with you.

I thank my viewers and readers who have loved me without even knowing me. I thank you for choosing me and for choosing this book. I hope you'll find this story the best I've told.

NOTES

CHAPTER 1: A MILLION CHANCES TO SAY YES
1. Jason Aldean, "Fly Over States," songwriters Neil Thrasher/Michael Dulaney, copyright © 2010 Sweet Summer Music/BMG Gold Songs (ASCAP); Major Bob Music, Inc., (ASCAP); Circle C Songs/Mojave Rain Music (Administered by Full Circle Music Publishing LLC) ASCAP. From the album *My Kinda Party*, copyright © 2010 This Is Hit, Inc., d/b/a Broken Bow Records.

CHAPTER 2: TAKE ME TO CHURCH
1. "Jim Downing: Navigator #6," navigators.org, August 1, 2015, https://www.navigators.org/jim-downing-navigator-6/.

CHAPTER 3: TUESDAY PEOPLE
1. Jeremiah 15:16, NLT.
2. John 3:16.

CHAPTER 4: A PIECE OF THE STORY
1. Jim relayed this story and these details to me personally in our conversations. You can also find this story in his memoir, *The Other Side of Infamy: My Journey through Pearl Harbor and the World of War* (Colorado Springs: NavPress, 2016).

CHAPTER 5: IN THE FISHBOWL
1. Proverbs 23:7, NKJV, paraphrased.

CHAPTER 6: ONE HUNDRED YEARS
1. Scripture quoted from the ESV.

CHAPTER 9: MARRIAGE TALK
1. Maxwell Maltz, *Psycho-Cybernetics* (New York: Pocket Books, 1969), 57–58.
2. At the time of writing, the number of births per second is now closer to 4.43; see https://ourworldindata.org/births-and-deaths.
3. Jim said this in one of our interviews. I'm not sure where he gleaned this fact.

CHAPTER 11: NEW LIFE
1. This tablet may not have existed (see https://quoteinvestigator .com/2012/10/22/world-end/), but it made a strong anecdote.

CHAPTER 12: SO LONG, DEAR FRIEND
1. Scripture quoted from the ESV.
2. This quote is commonly attributed to Epictetus.
3. Jim was paraphrasing Balzac here: "A conviction brings a salient indefinable beauty into faces made of the commonest human clay." Honoré de Balzac, *La Comédie humaine: The Country Parson and Albert Savaron*, trans. Ellen Marriage and Clara Bell (Philadelphia: Gebbie Publishing, 1898), 101.
4. See 1 Thessalonians 4:13-17.